CATS

EUGENIA NATOLI

CATS

Illustrations by Piero Cozzaglio

W.H. ALLEN · LONDON
1988

© 1987 Arnoldo Mondadori Editore S.p.A., Milan

© 1987 English translation by Arnoldo Mondadori Editore S.p.A., Milan

Produced by ERVIN s.r.l., Rome
under the supervision of ADRIANO ZANNINO

Editorial Assistant SERENELLA GENOESE ZERBI

Pen and ink drawings: Carlo Giordana, Andreina Scanu, Valeria Matricardi

Pencil drawings: Cecilia Giovannini

Photographs: © Eugenia Natoli

Text by Claudia Angeletti: The cat in art – Famous cats – The cat in
literature – The cat and music – The cat and the sea – The animated
cartoon cat – The comic strip cat – The cat in heraldry – The cat in
advertising

First British edition 1988

Translated by Ardèle Dejey

Printed and bound in Italy by
Officine Grafiche di Arnoldo Mondadori Editore, Verona
for the Publishers, W.H. Allen & Co. Plc
44 Hill Street, London W1X 8LB

ISBN 0-491-03188-2

Contents

INTRODUCTION

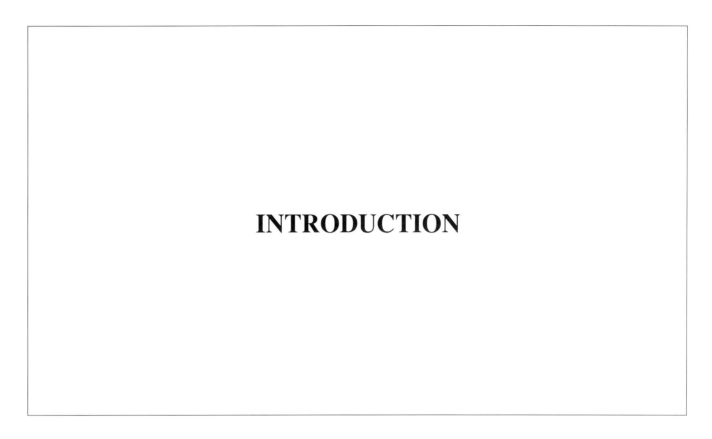

The cat is one of the best known animals, and perhaps the most beloved by man. Its large, unsmiling eyes, and the combination of the wild and the ambiguously sweet nature of the animal may explain the fascination the cat holds for many of us. And yet we know comparatively little about the cat and its origins, of the whys and wherefores of the countless "breeds," and of the bases for the characteristics – hereditary or acquired – of feline behaviour.

This book, unlike many others devoted to the subject, is more than just a catalogue of the various breeds of domestic cat, with advice on how to look after them; it also delves into the history of the cat's evolution, explores the labyrinthine subject of genetic variability, providing basic information on the variations of coat colour and pattern, as well as discussing the general conformation of the various types of domestic cat. In the last section – possibly the most interesting to the layman – the author deals with various aspects of feline behaviour, showing the extent to which the domestic cat's habits can be traced back to its wild ancestor and how this sheds light on the significance of its adaptations in evolutionary terms. Such characteristic behaviour includes marking and defense of territory, certain aspects of parental care (for example, the frequent transferring of the kittens by the mother to different "safe" places shortly after she has given birth, and the wide range of infantile behaviour patterns, much of which persists into adulthood.

A separate chapter deals with the development of the cat's social behaviour patterns, from its solitary ancestral forms to today's domestic cat, with its semi-social groups established in almost every large city. In these pages, for the most part the fruit of the author's own research work in the field, the life of the so-called "stray" is revealed to us in all its unsuspected complexity. The cat is one of the very few species in which the emergence of a social order is evolving almost before our eyes, with the appearance of group territorialism, the development of a hierarchical structure, and the first signs of the division of labour between members of the group.

Even the more technical aspects of the subject are explained plainly and simply which, together with the lively and charming illustrations, make for highly entertaining and informative reading. By the end, many mysteries will have been solved, but many new questions will emerge, which is surely the aim of every good book.

Prof. **Luciano Bullini**
Professor of Ecology and Animal Behaviour
University of Rome

7

The cat
in history

The cat is a beautiful and elegant animal. There are many who would agree with this statement. And, like all beautiful things, the cat does not leave man indifferent, but provokes extremes of emotion, either making him love it with utter devotion or hate it relentlessly. But whether it arouses feelings of antipathy, even utter loathing, or feelings of most tender affection, one particular fact remains: aesthetically, scarcely anyone finds it ugly. No other animal in the history of man has experienced such vagaries of fortune as the cat, which has not been without consequences. Indeed, it is almost impossible to reconstruct precisely the historical dates and events that link the life of the feline to that of man, so many are the legends, hovering on the verge between reality and fantasy, that revolve around it.

A reconstruction built about a degree of truth is possible only on broad lines. For example, the cat has been the subject of many treatises on the part it played in the civilization of Ancient Egypt and, later, in medieval Europe. It is also likely, however, that it has occupied an important rôle, of which relatively little is known, in the folkloric traditions of many other civilizations, centers of cultural diffusion since antiquity, such as India, China or Japan.

In the future more light will undoubtedly be shed on what is already known about the origins and genetic descent of the domestic cat. Modern research techniques are able to establish with ever greater accuracy the degree of the mixing of genes in today's domestic cat, to determine from which wild felines these genes come, and from which areas these animals originated.

From the historical point of view, it is important to look at all the information and references available and, without either believing in them blindly or discarding certain material out of hand, to examine the documentation with a critical eye. Let us look at a few examples: in fragments of ancient Mochica pottery (or Moche as they are sometimes called), those primitive Indians from the Andes from whom the Inca civilization sprang, men are depicted in the semblance of cats (or cats in the semblance of men?), engaged in a variety of activities: farming, practising medicine or playing musical instruments. Interesting information, certainly, but providing insufficient detail or concrete evidence for an in-depth study of the subject.

Evidence from Ancient Egypt testifying to the importance of the domesticated cat is more tangible and documented: finds of mummified cats, pictorial evidence and sculpture provide more accurate dates.

The cat's entry into Egyptian civilization can be dated with almost guaranteed certainty to 3000 B.C. At first the animal was treated as a divinity. Among the many Egyptian gods was one named Bast (or Bastet or Pash) which had a woman's body and the head of a cat. She was the goddess of fecundity and beauty, symbol of the sun, of light and of the moon. The Egyptians ac-

The cat as seen in a fresco from a tomb at Menna (XVIII Dynasty).

Cat on a lead: detail from an Egyptian wall painting.

Cat herding a group of ducks (Egyptian Museum, Cairo).

corded such importance to this cat-headed goddess that even real cats, seen as living symbols of this divinity, were held in high esteem. For the first time in the history of this part of the world the cat became a symbol of the era, divested of its guise of a wild, unapproachable creature, and entered man's home as part of the household, giving to the people the feeling that a divinity had finally descended from a throne to communicate with mortals. A divinity, in short, not cold and distant to be worshipped with humility and timid reverence as was customary with the gods, but one that was tangible and close.

In the end it was the cat's expertise as a rat-catcher that finally convinced the Egyptians of the animal's divine nature. The granaries at the time had become so large that they enabled enormous numbers of rodents to thrive (except, of course, among nomadic tribes that did not cultivate or store grain in huge quantities). The economic damage they caused was enormous. The advent of the domesticated feline, which kept the scourge under control, was seen as a further sign of its divine benevolence. Nor were the cat's physical qualities underrated, lending itself, as it does, to the perfect impersonation of a god: it is clean and ele-

The cat in art

The first pictorial representations of the cat are Egyptian and date from around 3000 B.C. The cat is shown with a hunting party in a marsh, springing out of the boat to seize a bird while clutching two others between his paws. Other pictures date from Roman times. Cats appear in some Pompeian frescoes and in a Roman mosaic, and it is a known fact that on the standards and shields of Roman legionaries cats were depicted as the symbol of independence.

During the Middle Ages the cat frequently appeared in bas-reliefs in churches, and at Moissac in France a cat and her kittens are carved on a capital.

In Renaissance art the cat had an obvious symbolical meaning. Ghirlandaio and Luini painted a cat at the feet of Judas, and Dürer used the animal as a symbol of evil in his *Adam and Eve* in which the cat is shown curling its tail around the woman's ankles as she stands by the tree of knowledge.

Leonardo da Vinci made some very beautiful sketches of cats in motion and his painting of the *Madonna with the cat* returns to a naturalistic portrayal

of the animal. Rembrandt, Bruegel, Veronese and Tintoretto included it as part of the background detail, serving to create an atmosphere of intimacy as in Barocci's *Annunciation*, in which a cat is asleep in a chair. Marie-Antoinette's court painter, Louise Elisabeth Vigée-Lebrun, included a cat dozing by the fire in her *Holy Family*.

In *The Sick Cat*, which depicts a doctor with serious expression treating a mouser assisted by its anxious mistress, Watteau introduced a new note: the cat is the focal point of the picture, and many artists from the Impressionists and Picasso to contemporary painters and line artists, such as Steinlen and Foujita, have sought to capture the fascination of this uncommon subject.

The Musée de l'Art Naïf in Paris celebrated the Year of the Cat in 1983 by putting on an exhibition; it was a huge success. The infinite possibilities of representation of this theme were amply illustrated, from sentimental or romantic portraits to more dramatic scenes, such as the rescuing of a small cat from the top of a building by firemen, with all the people looking upward.

Above: Roman mosaic from Pompeii, first century B.C. (Museo Nazionale, Naples). Below left: The cat at the foot of the tree of knowledge, in Dürer's engraving *Adam and Eve*; below right: Manet, lithograph for *Les Chats* by Jules Husson, 1870.

Marc Chagall, *Paris par la fenêtre* (detail), Guggenheim Museum, New York.

The cat as portrayed by two great painters: above, oil painting by Manet; left, drawing by Picasso.

Opposite: *Portrait of Pierre Loti* (1892) by Henri Rousseau ("le Douanier").

Left: the Cheshire Cat from Tenniel's illustration for *Alice in Wonderland*. Right: *Puss in Boots* by Grandville for Perrault's fairy tale. Below: Pinocchio's cat by Carlo Chiostri.

Famous cats

The cat is the protagonist of many stories starting with Aesop's fables and those of La Fontaine in which the animal is used allegorically to illustrate human failings.

In popular fables the cat is often gifted with a special kind of wisdom lacking in man. Yet although it is granted the powers of speech it is not portrayed as a magical creature: it is always a cat and, as such, knows instinctively how to deal with every kind of situation. Occasionally it is the link with that enchanted land that lies beyond the threshold of reality, not least for the air of mystery that has always surrounded it.

These are precisely the salient features of the two most famous cats of our childhood: Puss in Boots, who succeeded by cunning, and Alice's Cheshire Cat, who could appear and disappear at will.

Pinocchio's cat is a mirror of human hypocrisy, and yet it is first and foremost just an unfortunate animal that lives as it can, surviving against all odds, like the many cats you might see on street corners.

In almost all cat stories the subject of food arises, one of the most important priorities for our four-footed hero. Even when the star of the story is in fact a real-life prince under a spell, like the handsome white cat in Madame Aulnoy's *Tale of Blondine, Bonne-Biche and Beau-Minon*, while he takes on a feline form he also has feline interests. One of the most vividly drawn parts of this story is the description of all the food: "In front of Bonne-Biche there was a small stool for Beau-Minon, before him a golden bowl filled to the brim with little fried fish and woodcocks' legs; nearby a crystal basin full of the freshest milk," and the description varies each evening according to the story-teller's whim, to the delight no doubt of young listeners.

The proletarian cat belonging to Pinocchio is quite different; he eats a modest supper at the Red Crab Inn: "The poor cat, feeling seriously unwell with stomach-ache, could eat nothing but thirty-five red mullet with a gant; it has a mysterious and captivating expression; its eyes are no ordinary colour but seem to reflect the brilliance of precious stones: jade, amethysts, sapphires, emeralds. It has the necessary agility to vanish instantly into nothingness, as though it had never been in the place it was occupying a few seconds before – all characteristics capable of exciting the imagination of those who choose to see the supernatural, even where it does not exist. These same characteristics, differently interpreted and therefore arousing fear, have caused the cat to be condemned in times past. In Egypt it was prized to the extent of being worshipped as a god; it was fed, housed, respected and caressed. Unless by accident or in fights with other animals the cat never died by violent means, but was left to grow old peacefully. Accidental deaths were rare, not only because the widespread love for the animal made people particularly cautious in their treatment of it, but also because killing a cat was a crime punishable by death. Members of a family whose cat had died shaved off their eyebrows as a sign of mourning. All kinds of tribute were paid to the dead cat as if it were a real member of the household; it was embalmed, wrapped in costly, coloured bandages and placed in a magnificent sarcophagus. Even rats were embalmed and

Bronze statue of the goddess Bastet (Ashmolean Museum, Oxford).

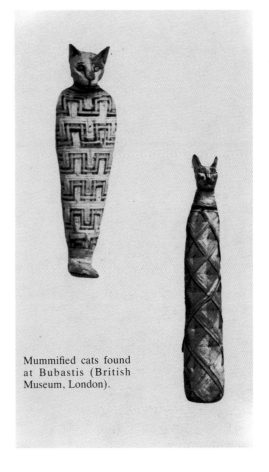

Mummified cats found at Bubastis (British Museum, London).

tomato salad and four portions of tripe with parmesan cheese; and because he thought the tripe was not well seasoned he went back three times to ask for butter and grated cheese."

Finally, there is Gottfried Keller's cat Spiegel ("Mirror") who makes a pact with a sorcerer who uses cat fat for his spells. For three months Spiegel eats as much as he can, then he is to sacrifice himself in the name of science. There follows a description of the cat's gargantuan meals of strings of sausages, spiced salamis and *Würstel* which are pulled out of a big pot by the hundred, steaming and dripping with fat, or fried golden brown, bursting apart to reveal their rosy, succulent meat to the hungry cat. Of course, after the three months Spiegel uses his cunning to save his skin and goes on his way, fat and sleek. Hence the Austrian saying "to think you have bought the cat's fat" meaning that one has been taken for a ride.

Cats have inspired the strangest stories. In William Rose Bénet's *The King of the Cats* a curious conductor who is the rage of New York actually conducts with his tail.

Today, cats in stories wear different clothes and move in a more real world. The heroine of William Mayne's *The Patchwork Cat* loves the milkman more than anything in the world, and watches out for him every morning. She also loves an old patchwork quilt which, to her horror, is thrown out because it is so dirty. In her efforts to get it back, Tabby ends up in a rubbish bin and is carried off by the rubbish truck. This is the beginning of an adventurous journey; Tabby finally recovers her quilt and takes it back to the house. She sleeps until midday then opens an eye, stretches, makes sure she is at home and falls asleep again for the rest of the afternoon.

But not all cats are as conventional as this. In Rodari's *Vado via con i gatti* (Leaving to join the cats), Signor Antonio, a retired station master, takes himself off to live with the cats at Torre Argentina because no one in his family can be bothered with him. He discovers to his surprise that other people there have also turned into cats. There's a dustman who has run away from an old people's home, a few lonely old ladies tyrannized by their housemaids, even a judge who would seem to have had everything in life: a beautiful home, a happy family, a secure position, but who obviously prefers Torre Argentina. When the cats' mothers arrive with their bags of food, he takes his share and goes off to eat it on the top step of a temple. In the evenings the cats have lessons in astronomy and are, in short, content with their lot.

In a prayer to the Creator which ends his collection of subtle and witty verses, *Il gatto romano* (The Roman Cat) Mario Dell'Arco, writes: "God, if you wish to reincarnate me in a future life, as an animal, I beg you, take notice of my character, my habits, my inclinations, and make me a cat."

Bas-relief of the Battle of Marathon showing a cat on a lead, fifth century B.C.

placed beside the cat so that it would not go hungry on its journey to the other world, proving that the Egyptians believed in an afterlife even for the cat. In 1890, about 300,000 mummified cats were found in a state of perfect preservation among the ruins of the ancient Egyptian city of Bubastis. Unfortunately most were destroyed. At the time, when the importance of scientific research was not fully appreciated, it was thought better to use the mummies as manure, and such was their unhappy end.

After the decline of Egyptian civilization the cat continued for a time to enjoy many privileges, even in other countries, because of its invaluable skill as a rat-catcher. Indeed, even those who, for various reasons, used to destroy cats, were forced to admit their error and change their ways when unforeseen population explosions among rodents were acknowledged as the cause of devastating damage to health and economy: at various times in the past bubonic plague claimed thousands of victims without ever being conquered.

It would appear that the cat was brought to Europe by the Greeks who, having discovered its prowess as a hunter, had at first tried to persuade the Egyptians to sell it to them. When they did not succeed, because obviously, a goddess could not be bought or sold, the Greeks decided to steal the animals.

The Romans also prized the cat as a hunter, but no more than that. Neither the Greeks nor the Romans ever worshipped it as a deity, unlike other peoples of the past, or other religions and civilizations, such as the Hindus for example. Even today, a good Hindu must feed at least one cat during the course of his life.

In China too, where the cat appeared around 1000 B.C., it was very fortunate: it became a symbol of family happiness and to it some Chinese attributed divine powers. From China the highly honoured traveller continued his happy journey on to Japan and came ashore around the year A.D. 999.

To the Japanese the cat was a noble animal worthy of every attention, and they

did not therefore employ it as a rat-catcher. And so Japan too suffered heavy economic losses (especially in silkworm breeding), as a result of rodents multiplying uncontrollably. With truly astonishing ingenuity the Japanese decided to fill their towns and cities with statues and drawings of cats, believing that the rats would flee before these images of their great enemy. Not surprisingly, this stratagem failed to produce the desired effect. It was not until 1620, more than six hundred years after the cat's first appearance in Japan, that it was let off its leash and allowed to hunt freely.

At the same time in other parts of the world the cat was suffering very harsh treatment, paying the price for having been worshipped by many pagan peoples. Around A.D. 1200 the cat fell into disgrace among all those under the dominance of the Christian Church, and was condemned as the very incarnation of paganism against which the Church was battling unremittingly. It is a kind of irony that, in order to condemn the cat, the Church resorted to weapons worthy

The cat in literature

T he cat's relationship with poets could not but be full of emotion: "Viens, mon beau chat/sur mon coeur amoureux" wrote Baudelaire in his poem, *Le Chat*. And one must surely be touched by the melancholy in the verses of Torquato Tasso, alone and ill in hospital; he turned to the only creatures who consoled his last years and lit up the darkness of his mind, by this time already very disturbed: "O, cat/light of my studies/O, beloved cat."

Let us recall the somewhat ribald animals in Lope de Vega's burlesque epic about cats *Gatomaquia* (1634). How closely he must have observed the feline world to describe so well the beautiful Zapaquilda who sits on top of a tall chimney pot in a cool wind, busy licking herself from the top of her head to the tip of her tail, with the meticulousness and hauteur of a convent cat, "and her own mind serves as a mirror," or the proud Marrasmaquis who, in spouting abuse at his rival who is trying to snatch from him the beauty, will not let go of a pie which he has seized and holds on to as tightly as a drowning man would an oar.

The same themes recur in the pages dedicated by many famous writers to cats, from Théophile Gautier, Colette, and Anatole France to Gina Lagorio with her *Tosca dei gatti*, to name but a few. Other writers have even suggested a metaphysical element behind man's fascination for the cat (and which could be the reason for the irrational hatred felt by others toward the animal). Swinburne wrote: "Stately, kindly, lordly friend/Condescend/Here to sit by me, and turn/Glorious eyes that smile and burn,/Golden eyes, love's lustrous meed,/On the golden page I read." And Lytton Strachey: "Dear creature by the fire a-purr,/Strange idol, eminently bland,/Miraculous puss! As

o'er your fur/I trail a negligible hand."

The cat, indeed, has a place of his own in general books and in anthologies. The first include Champfleury's *Les Chats* of 1870, and *Our Cats* written in 1889 by the famous English illustrator Harrison Weir. A great lover of cats, Weir organized the first major cat show in London at the Crystal Palace in July 1871.

Brunner and Hlawaceck enjoyed overwhelming success with their book on how to understand the cat and make oneself understood by it. This was basically a scientific work but it also answered the endless list of questions asked by all cat owners. Brunner was a veterinary surgeon who had opened a clinic thirty years earlier in Vienna; he was the city's first ever animal psychologist and explained to pet owners how to treat the repressed instinct developed in cats that were forced to live in small apartments.

Also of interest is a text originally written for fun and which then became a milestone in the field: in the nineteenth century a Lombard doctor and man of letters, Giovanni Rajberti, wrote a learned philosophical essay on the cat in which he compares human behaviour with that of felines, concluding that the cat is vastly superior. A keen animal observer, Rajberti wrote, quite unwittingly, what was to become the first serious scientific study on the habits and psychology of cats.

of pagans, namely the mixing of magic with religion – the only way to impress the ignorant populace – to nurture and spread among them the belief that cats were witches transformed into animals, that they were creatures from Hell, possessed of demonic powers and that, as such, they were to be destroyed.

Poor cats! How could they be defended from these calumnies at such a time of obscurantism and ignorance, in which superstition was rife, fed by those in power since it is always easier to rule by fear. The very fact that cats' eyes glowed in the dark was sufficient for diabolic powers to be attributed to them. And it was not only the cat who paid such a heavy price: many women were tried and burnt at the stake as witches and, at times, the sole charge that condemned the victim to such a dreadful death was that she kept a cat. When there was no woman to be accused of witchcraft a trial was set in motion in which the prisoner in the dock was a cat. Clearly the animal could say nothing in its own defense, and even if it

Another well-known book, *How to Live with a Calculating Cat* by Eric Gurney, presents a precise analysis in a humorous, though rigorously scientific tone of the man-cat relationship. Recently, Stephen Baker has added to the list with *How to Live with a Neurotic Cat*, which makes up for the lack of amusing illustrations found in Gurney, by the strength of its observation.

According to Baker, these are some of the things a cat gets up to in the house to pass the day innocently. The broom: chew its bristles; the vacuum cleaner: pull out the bag and watch the dust fly about; the pressure cooker: squeeze inside for forty winks; the rubbish bin: pull off the lid, strew the contents across the floor and feast on any leftovers.

Here also are a few minutes of a cat's typical evening. Time 6.40: his master sits in an armchair to read the newspaper; the cat settles himself on the back of the chair; time 6.41: his master sends the cat packing; time 6.42: the cat jumps up again; time 6.45: his master chases away the cat and sits on the sofa, again attempting to read the paper; time 6.46: the cat follows him and jumps on his lap; time 6.47: his master pushes him off; time 6.48: the cat jumps down, tearing the newspaper in two.

It is clear that the author is intimately acquainted with cats; perhaps he has one of his own.

Often associated with feminine characteristics, the cat is portrayed here in women's clothes by Grandville: top, *"The fashionable beauty"* from *Poor Minette*; above: *"Come, Minette, the world is at your feet."*

could it would have been futile since the only possible outcome of the trial was for the accused, whether cat or woman, to be put to death. Where it was convenient the cat, paradoxically, became the emblem of the Church itself, in order to justify burning it publicly. In Catholic England the cat was the symbol of Protestantism; in Protestant England the symbol of Catholicism.

To complicate matters the cat had always been associated in one form or another with feminine characteristics which, in view of the times, was certainly no help to its popularity because of the distrust with which women were regarded, being considered as potential witches. One of the most serious consequences of these feline trials and executions was that at the time Europe's population was being decimated by the plague, spread by rats which were free to reproduce and increase without hindrance. Such events did nothing to lessen the fanatical attitudes adopted against the cat, which lasted for hundreds of years. It was not until after the

The Japanese frequently depict the cat with one raised paw, after the legend of the Shinjuku temple cat (temple painting, Tokyo).

French Revolution that the situation began to change; however, the barbarous practice involving various forms of torture to cats in order to drive away the "evil eye" from people's houses did not stop.

Even in the present century, in which scientific research has advanced sufficiently to provide definitive explanations for the causes of many phenomena which at one time were thought to be supernatural, at a stage in man's history then, which finds little room for superstition, it is still believed that black cats bring good luck. There is no justification whatsoever for beliefs of this kind: the study of genetics has explained once and for all that a cat is born black and not white because its genes are those for the colour black. Old habits and beliefs die hard; the only weapon with any chance of success is education. A careful study should therefore be made of the historical evidence for these two rôles – of the cat as a goddess of propitiation, and of the cat as the incarnation of destructive evil. And yet these rôles have

The cat and music

In ancient Egypt, as well as the goddess Bastet, there was another deity with a cat's head: the god of music. The connection is not so strange when one remembers that the cat is extremely sensitive to sound and loves music. In spite of this it has not inspired many compositions: Domenico Scarlatti's *Cat Fugue*; Rossini's *Duetto buffo per due gatti* (Comic Duet for Two Cats); Ravel's orchestral cat sounds in

L'Enfant et les Sortilèges, which gave him considerable worry: he asked his librettist Colette if he could change *mouae* for *mouain*; Stravinsky's *Owl and the Pussycat* (to words by Edward Lear); the scene with the White Cat and Puss in Boots from Tchaikovsky's ballet *The Sleeping Beauty*, in which the orchestra reproduce mewing and spitting, and only a few others.

In the United States and Britain recently, the musical *Cats* by Andrew Lloyd Webber, has scored an enormous hit. It is based on T.S. Eliot's book *Old Possum's Book of Practical Cats* in which the cat "who sits and sits and sits and sits" has a part: she sits "Beside the hearth or in the sun or in my hat . . . she sits upon the window-sill or anything that's smooth and flat." However, " . . . when all the family's in bed and asleep,/She tucks up her skirts to the basement to creep" and she likes to wind the curtain-cord and "tie it into sailor-knots."

The cinema has popularized much of the theme music for films, among which is the already classic plush-covered step of "The Pink Panther."

Right: musical notations representing cats in this Schubert score. Opposite: poster by Steinlen for the *Chat noir* cabaret (1896).

something in common: throughout the centuries the cat has always possessed a certain magical quality. Scientific knowledge has allowed us to divest it of its magical guise, giving back to it its proper dignity and recognizing it as an animal that simply roams the streets, or is loved as a member of the family.

During the nineteenth century studies of animal behaviour developed apace and interest in ethology involved even those outside the field. For a long time students neglected the cat, thinking it of little relevance in their studies of wildlife in view of its status as a domesticated animal. Unfortunately cats were widely used instead for anatomical and physiological studies. Now it has returned once again to the limelight, ethological interest having been reawakened by the growing numbers of strays living on the streets, leading players in behavioural phenomena for which no explanation has yet been found. The cat again succeeds in surrounding itself with mystery.

The First Stage of Cruelty, engraving by Hogarth in which cats are shown being tortured.

The cat and the sea

The first time the cat went to sea was indisputably in Noah's Ark. Allegedly it was born as Noah stepped on board, from a lion's sneeze, and served to control the mice which plundered the provisions. For this reason two cats were always kept on board ships; the more beautiful, usually ginger, belonged to the captain.

But their usefulness was not limited to hunting rodents; they were believed to bring luck for a safe voyage. Furthermore, sailors were able to tell a great deal from the cats' behaviour; if they washed their faces with their paws or sneezed, rain could be expected; if they clawed at cloth or clung to the sail, a storm would blow up; if they began to play, a fair wind would follow. If the sailors wanted the wind to change then the cat had to be shut inside a cooking pot. Most of these beliefs can be explained by the cat's almost barometric sensitivity to the elements. Before rain a cat becomes restless and sometimes tries to hide. There were other superstitions: to throw a cat overboard would cause a storm; to kick it would give you rheumatism, and drowning it was supposed to bring the devil upon you.

The most famous cat ever to set sail was Fitzy, the main character in an English fairy tale. He belonged to a very poor boy, Dick Whittington, who in the fourteenth century went to sea as a cabin-boy, sailing to the Indies. The ship was wrecked on a cannibal island infested with rats and here Fitzy proved his worth by killing all the rats and saving the lives of all the crew.

He was immediately made a general and his master became the cannibal king's minister. Years later the two, by now very rich, returned to London and Dick was made Lord Mayor. He kept the nickname of Lord Cat and was certainly not offended by it.

Eliot's cats

Thomas Stearns Eliot understood cats. He "felt" everything which, in a cat, is indescribable and, even more unusual, succeeded through his words in making the public understand the essence of the feline: a being-non being, happily described in his collection of poems on cats, *Old Possum's Book of Practical Cats*, published in 1939.

Although this work has been translated into many languages there is always the difficulty with a language as diverse as English, in trying to express the original idea. "Possum" means "opossum," a small marsupial of the kangaroo family which inhabits America. "Possum" was also Eliot's nickname to his friends.

In translating the title of the work into a foreign language there is a problem from the very outset in how to render the word "practical." Should it be taken to mean "sensible," "useful" or "proper" in the sense of "real" – all possible translations of "practical?"

Each poem is a play on words and the fun begins with the fantastic names involved for cats in general: Jellicle cats, and for each one in particular: Jennyanydots, Growltiger, Griddlebone, Rum Tum Tugger, Macavity, Mungojerrie and Rumpleteaser, to name but a few.

Eliot knew exactly how to capture the essence of "catness" (it would be more proper to say "felinity") with the very first name "Jellicle": it sounds like jelly, and jelly conjures up a picture of brightness, luminosity, shining; shining moon, "jellicle moon."

His understanding of the mystery and reserve of cats reveals itself in the first poem on their names: *The Naming of Cats*. It is not easy to give a name to a cat: Eliot says that it is not a "holiday game," especially because the cat needs more than one name. The first is the one "that the family use daily . . . all of them sensible everyday names" without pretention; the second must be "particular" and "peculiar, and more dignified" and belong to only one cat, a name of such importance that the cat can "cherish his pride" and keep "his tail perpendicular/Or spread out his whiskers"; and the third is the name that no human will ever discover because only a cat can choose his own name in the course of "profound meditation," a name defined by Eliot as "His ineffable, effable/Effanineffable/Deep and inscrutable singular name."

And the play on words in the names themselves continues. He had the ability to define in one word the most salient traits of a personality. His subjects are cat-cats and cat-humans, but more cat than human, unlike in the past when cats represented only human characters, such as in Aesop's *Fables*, and those of the Latin fabulist Phaedrus. Eliot wrote about cats he had observed: the poem on the terrible pair of spoil-sports, Mungojerrie and Rumpelteaser, tells of two inseparable, good-for-nothing friends whose main occupation is organizing smash-and-grab raids with a skill that is purely cat-like. It is, of course, quite natural to identify these two characters with human subjects but, as we read Eliot's verses, we are completely drawn into the world of the cat, entertained by the feats described such as the stealing of the Sunday roast from the oven, reducing the house to a battlefield or smashing the vase "commonly said to be Ming," then vanishing from the scene of the crime with a mystifying skill common to cats but not men. The author sent this poem to his little niece with the apology that perhaps it was not very good because " . . . the two cats described are in the end much worse in reality than he was able to imagine."

Different parts of the book make the reader smile, either because he recognizes his own qualities and weaknesses in the personages described or, equally, because they are strange to him. Before his eyes marches past the "Bravo Cat," the terror of the Thames, Growltiger, a tabby who, when "the tender moon was shining bright," serenaded his beautiful Griddlebone, unaware of the danger surrounding his barge. His enemies, the Siamese, the moonlight reflected from "their thousand bright blue eyes," storm his barge and force him to walk the plank as he had forced a hundred others. (Griddlebone escapes.) Other characters include the efficient Jennyanydots who organizes music lessons and crocheting for the mice, as well as drilling the cockroaches into a troop of helpful boy-scouts; and Old Deuteronomy (the fifth book of the Bible), the old wise cat of the village, respected by everyone and never disturbed even when he chooses to sit in the middle of the High Street on market day causing chaos . . . and so on.

There is also the game with the readers having their legs pulled: once again Eliot depicts cats as beings-non beings, sense-no sense, understandable with difficulty by man. His poem, the *Ad-dressing of Cats* poses the conclusive question: what is a cat? The author humorously replies " . . . A CAT IS NOT A DOG" and "A Dog's a Dog – A CAT'S A CAT." And, more seriously, he reminds us that to understand a cat we must respect his reserve and offer him true friendship. Only then (and here he jokes again) can one hope to achieve one's aim: to "finally call him by his NAME" . . . "his ineffable effable/Effanineffable/Deep and inscrutable singular Name."

The cat and dance

One of the greatest challenges a dancer can face is to perform a dance that recreates the physical flexibility of an animal far more lithe than mere humans – an animal as supple and acrobatic as a cat. Yet Andrew Lloyd Webber has attempted and achieved exactly this.

With the help of an exceptional team of choreographers, directors, lighting and sound technicians, musicians and singer-dancer-actors, he created the musical *Cats*, which had its London première in 1981, and is still enjoying world-wide success.

It was certainly no mean feat but who, if not he – the author of *Jesus Christ Superstar* (1970), *Evita* (1975) and many other successful musicals – could have brought it off? In most of his stage hits the lyrics are written to fit the music composed by Webber, but in *Cats* the opposite was the case: as far as was possible, Webber left unaltered the text of T.S. Eliot's *Old Possum's Book of Practical Cats*, and adapted his music to the verse. His task was made easier by the fact that the original verse was already extraordinarily musical and, although a few slight alterations were necessary, the rhythm of the text itself actually inspired Webber in his composition.

Since it first became domesticated the cat has appeared in art in varied forms: poets, painters, sculptors, writers and musicians have all drawn inspiration from what is perhaps the world's most celebrated animal. To describe it in words, images or sounds means knowing how to capture its most striking features and how to represent them in a different form: but man remains man and cat remains cat.

To describe it through movement, on the other hand, involves the challenge of imitating the animal, and it is in achieving exactly this that has brought success to the show: humans cease to be human beings and become cats. Only the techniques of contemporary dance could produce such spectacular effects. Once again the cat has found a place in artistic expression: in *Cats* it becomes the protagonist in a spectacle of modern dance. After all, dance is perhaps the most appropriate form of artistic expression for this animal. Are not the movements of a cat possibly its most characteristically feline attribute?

This is what has been asked of the dancers in *Cats*: to recreate the very essence of feline qualities, to be reserved, and at the same time extremely sensual, hot, cold, complete, elastic and mysterious as only cats can be, and to translate all this into a spirited theatrical spectacle, into a

Programme illustration for the musical *Cats* by Andrew Lloyd Webber.

crescendo which presents to the audience the atmosphere which pervades Eliot's poem, the now lost atmosphere of London in the thirties.

Through the incidents in the lives of the now famous Jennyanydots (the efficient cat), Growltiger (the pirate cat), Deuteronomy (the wise old cat), Mungojerrie and Rumpelteaser (the infernal, kill-joy friends), Macavity (the mysterious cat) and many others, the audience enters into the world of cats, and they laugh, love and suffer with them. It is a world of dark alleys, of the banks of the Thames, of rooftops and houses, but above all of the street that is the real theater of a cat's life. The audience's involvement surely reaches its climax when Grizabella, the cat who was once enchanting, now fallen into disgrace, sings of her grief.

The text of the song *Memory*, sung in the musical by Elaine Page but also well-known through Barbara Streisand's interpretation, was not published by Eliot in his book because he thought the story was too

sad for children. Grizabella is the drop-out who lives on memories, who yearns for contact, for a place in the community, but at whose appearance all flee, so sorry is her plight and her obvious unhappiness. All she can do is sit and talk in the frozen night to the frozen moon, reproaching it for having forgotten the days when she was "the glamour puss," the fascinating cat, loved and admired by all.

Here, then, we see cat-men, because the feline society depicted in the musical is clearly the mirror of human society; but then on the other hand we see cat-cats, because the dancers move and behave as cats. The extraordinary result is a direct link between the work of Eliot and that of the *Cats* team: reading the poetry or watching the show, two specifically human activities, truly increases our understanding of cats, because they both succeed in revealing the unmystified feline essence, creating the impression that the dancers are not men and women disguised as cats, but cats disguised as men and women.

The animated cartoon cat

Felix, Sylvester, Tom and Jerry were all intended for the animated cartoon rather than the comic strip. Indeed, they are highly dynamic characters created specifically for the cinema. In fact only animated drawings can do real justice to their comic acrobatics, to the complicated stratagems adopted by them to defeat the enemy or to purloin a pie, to the terrifying catastrophes which generally result from their misdemeanours, and also make possible escape into the absurd.

Walt Disney's characters, on the other hand, were developed first for the comic strip and then for cartoon films. We therefore see a continuous osmosis between comic strip and cartoon. Some characters only ever appear in one picture, such as the three little kittens in the cartoon *Three Orphan Kittens*; or Ambrose, the kitten who dreams of becoming a bandit; or the cat who disguises himself as Father Christmas to get into the mouse's den, but is discovered by a crafty little mouse who spots his tail sticking out from under the red cloak, and chases him away using toy soldiers and mechanical toys that the cat has brought as presents.

Later there are the cats of a few full-length Walt Disney films: the Cheshire Cat from *Alice in Wonderland* and the malicious Siamese cats from *Cinderella*, the wicked tormentors of the mice who are the heroes.

One cartoon in which cats do manage to get their revenge is *The Aristocats*, in which aristocratic cats such as the Duchess and her offspring, and proletarians like Romeo and his ragamuffin friends are portrayed sympathetically.

Other famous cats in Walt Disney's films are real life felines: the Siamese in *That Darn Cat* and the striped cat in *The Cat from Outer Space*.

The comic strip cat

The first comic strip cat was Herriman's Krazy Kat of 1911. She was an outlandish skinny tabby who spoke as though she had a cold because she was a German immigrant. She was in love with the wicked mouse Ignatz, who threw bricks at her all the time without this changing her romantic inclinations, and she was loved hopelessly by the police dog Offissa Pupp.

The opposite of this crazy creature was Pat Sullivan's adventurous vagabond Felix who "kept on walking, walking, walking, and he's walking all the time"; always struggling with adverse fate, like Chaplin's tramp, and always ready to help anyone in trouble. He appeared for the first time in 1923, but in fact made his début in the cinema as early as 1917. Felix brought to the comic strip that surrealist element which belongs to the cartoon, in which characters walk on air until they suddenly realize they have no means of support.

Felix, then, lived in a fantasy world in which everything was possible. He could solve any problem with his brilliant ideas: he steals a moon of yellow cheese for the grocer who has nothing left to sell (who is then arrested because people are left in the dark); he fills up the empty coal cellar with the notes that come out of a saxophone and freeze in the winter air; to an elderly couple

The cat in heraldry

Animals which symbolized courage and audacity in battle, such as the lion and the leopard, were much featured in heraldry. The image of the cat was also used by families in whose name the sound "cat" or "chat" occurred. The Scottish Chattan clan had a Scottish wild cat on its coat-of-arms; the Catesby family had a spotted cat. There is also a coat-of-arms in which a cat appears with a mouse in its mouth, possibly the one chosen by Dick Whittington who had a cat placed on his family escutcheon after becoming rich and powerful, thanks to his cat, Fitzy.

With the abolition of noble titles after the French Revolution, family coats-of-arms disappeared in France, but by a curious phenomenon were transferred to the doorways of shops and inns as signs. And on these signs, as also in the names of the premises, once again the cat appears: Top Cat *(Gros chat)*, The Laughing Cat *(Le chat qui rit)*, The Black Cat *(Le chat noir)*.

who have lost their canary he gives the twittering nestlings that appear in the air when he falls and hits his head. Felix became so popular in fact that Lindbergh chose him as the mascot for his aeronautical company.

In the world of Walt Disney cats are usually the local felines chased by Pluto, with the exception of Nip who belongs to the golden years of Mickey Mouse. Nip is an alley cat who, on more than one occasion, humiliates our hero by tying knots in his tail. When he is about to go on to knotting his nose, Mickey discovers catnip (catmint), a potion that inebriates cats, and reverses the situation.

But the great adversary is Peg-leg Pete, a fierce black cat, gangster by profession, whose path is always crossed by Mickey. Each adventure ends with the apparent defeat of Peg-leg, but he inevitably survives each scrape to return even more of a rascal than ever and even more determined to get his own back on the mouse. And so he sets about hatching new plots that will inevitably be thwarted by Mickey: a never-ending saga.

In the stories devised by Hanna and Barbera the battleground is contained within the four walls of the house. This is defended to the bitter end by the cat, Tom, against the intrusion of the two little mice who live in a hole in the wall. These are the enterprising Jerry and a tiny little baby mouse called Tuffy. When Tom is asleep the two mice regularly raid the kitchen and other rooms in search of food, or explore the delights of the house, where everything seems to have been made for their amusement. Their favourite game, however, is making a fool of the cat, laying traps for him and reducing his nerves to shreds. Almost without exception Tom ends up the loser.

Both characters were so successful that the magazine in which they appeared in 1942, *Our Gang*, changed its name to *Tom and Jerry*.

Another intriguing couple is Tweety, the canary, and Sylvester, a large black and white tomcat, of limited intelligence with a big, round nose. He spends most of his time working out ways and means of capturing Tweety. But Hector, the dog, keeps watch, and Tweety himself is not as guileless as he seems. Chasing him turns out to be a dangerous sport and Sylvester suffers a stream of knocks and blows that always leave him totally dazed: a truly pitiful case in which the victim is not the poor, defenseless little bird but the big, tough cat.

In 1978 a new character appeared in the United States who was destined to make all others pale by comparison. This was Jim Davis's feline friend Garfield. The series presents a portrait of a pet cat and his owner, Jon.

Garfield has a powerful personality: he completely dominates his master and gets whatever he wants, even resorting to violence if necessary. He is fat, lazy, deceitful and bad-tempered; he sleeps on his master's face, eats his turkey and ruins his furniture; yet no cat could be more tenderly loved, and without him Jon would feel lost. Garfield is in fact part of his life, and is his confidant and counsellor: although Garfield does not speak, he and Jon can understand each other with a mere glance.

The fact that millions of Americans identify with Jon and can see mirrored in Garfield the personality of their own cat guarantees the success of the character. Today his stories are published in at least 1,150 American dailies and he is also extremely well-known abroad.

A whole industry has sprung up around Garfield with a variety of commercial products including soft toys, greetings cards and books on the market. He has now become a symbol in his own right and his sarcastic sallies are proverbial, his favourite saying being "Cats are invincible."

Love and hate: Steinlen's famous cats.

The cat in advertising

Since the very beginnings of advertising the cat has been used to promote a wide variety of products, with the most tenuous of links.

One of the earliest examples was a publicity postcard showing a large black and white cat in an armchair looking very contented with life. In 1885 this was used in the States to advertise Old Tom Gin, a brand of English gin which had taken the name Tom from the word "tomcat".

The Catlin Tobacco Company, on the other hand, put its money on the cat because of its connection with the company name, and chose an unusual and pleasing image: a cat defending the Tobacco box with her kittens inside, hissing and arching her back. From then on the cat was traditionally used to promote cigars and tobacco.

Prominent among the many tobacco companies was Axton-Fisher who, in 1943, used the picture of a white

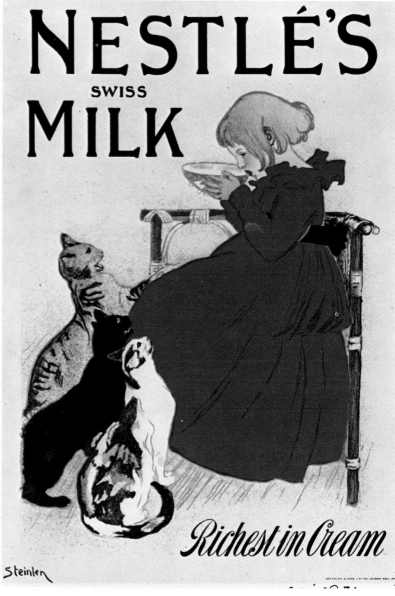

angora cat, licking itself meticulously, to launch filter-tip cigarettes. Among other advantages, these did not leave nicotine stains and, according to the advertisement, every puff on this cigarette was "self-cleansing."

Other goods promoted by the idea of cleanliness which was associated with the cat included soaps, talcum powder and a variety of household cleaning products. The most original advertising campaign was undoubtedly that for Mansion Polish. Their posters showed a kitten admiring its reflection in the surface of a piano, shining with Mansion's wax furniture polish, while the mother complacently contemplates her tail reflected in the highly polished floor, and exclaims: "If you want to check that your tail is in place, just look at yourself in a floor cleaned with Mansion polish."

Also used to promote quality products, the cat was chosen by Gold Starry of Paris, producers of the first fountain pens. The advertisement dates from 1915, and is in Art Nouveau style: a beautiful white cat, writing with a Gold Starry pen, says: "I no longer write like a cat," referring to a saying familiar to many European children, who are told that their bad writing is like that "of a cat."

The cat was also used in advertising during the Second World War. The Chesapeake and Ohio Railway Company created the characters of the kitten Chessie, and her friend Peake to advertise the sleeping car with the slogan "Sleep like a kitten." A 1944 calendar showed Peake, at the front, with a photograph of Chessie to hang by his bed, while the Company apolo-

gized to travellers for the fact that, in view of the times, Chessie and Peake could not be with them for a while: the cause must come first.

Many posters were works of art and became famous, such as Steinlen's poster for Nestlé's milk, showing a little girl holding a large bowl in her hands, surrounded by cats demanding their share. George Gibbs' poster for cream of wheat shows a cat greedily licking the pieces of broken bowl dropped by his young master. More recent cats include those used in Will Barnet's posters to advertise art exhibitions.

With the advent of television and cinema came real live cats in advertising, far less imaginative perhaps, but appealing nevertheless, generally employed to promote cat food and beauty products.

The evolution of the cat

The history of the cat is that of both demon and god, embodied in one animal. Or rather, it is the history of the opposing rôles that man has imposed on the cat: with the fickleness that distinguishes our own species, the cat has been placed on an altar and worshipped as a deity only to be persecuted later and burnt at the stake, as a demon with witches. But these are well known facts; the good fortune of the cat in ancient Egypt and its later fall from grace in the Middle Ages have been the subject of many treatises.

But what was the cat's history before Egyptian civilization, that is, in the period before its domestication? Who were the first representatives of the family Felidae from which our house cat descends, and what happened after the cat ceased to be tortured for being believed to be the incarnation of the devil?

Both periods, that preceding the cat's domestication and that following its persecution, have one banal but significant factor in common: in both the cat has simply been itself.

The evolutionary history of its progenitors begins at the end of the Cainozoic era, not less than two million years ago, and it is from that time that the differentiation between the genus *Felis* and the common lineage of the Felidae dates. The evolution of the domestic cat, *Felis catus*, dates back 5,000 years, when the process of domestication of its direct progenitor, the wildcat *Felis silvestris* first began. In the period between two million and 5,000 years ago, the forebears of the domestic cat were therefore simply cats, intermediary links (predators but also the prey of other animals) in the food chain of the ecosystem in which they lived.

From its entry into human history (about

The Ancient Egyptians believed the cat to be a reincarnation of the goddess Bastet.

3000 B.C.) to the beginning of the twentieth century, the cat has played many rôles and experienced the consequences of domestication: it has been venerated as a god, feared as the devil, hounded as a witch and loved as a child. Extrasensory and paranormal powers have even been attributed to the animal, and it was at one time believed that the cat was capable of predicting earthquakes.

In the twentieth century, it returned to being just a simple cat. The two factors responsible for this change of attitude are basically culture and prosperity. The spread of education to all social strata has finally dispelled the semi-religious, semi-magical aura with which popular folklore surrounded the cat for so long. For so many centuries such attitudes caused it to be attributed with the malevolence of the devil (in contrast to the benevolence of God), and with the occult power of sorcery, leading to its unfavourable association with magic phenomena.

In the space of just one century improved social well-being and education have led to a greater interest being taken in animals generally. On average, more money and time than ever before are now devoted to pets; but even in the breeding of rare or highly-prized species, whether as a hobby or as a full-time occupation, the cat is at last allowed to be simply a cat.

In this chapter we shall examine the life of the cat-as-cat or of the Felidae family when the cat as such did not yet exist in its present-day form, and then we shall go on to examine its function in modern society.

In order to understand the domestic cat, we must first analyse the physical and behavioural characteristics of its direct ancestor, the wildcat, *Felis silvestris* and the process of its domestication which has resulted in our modern-day *Felis catus*.

The cat family

n layman's terms the felids (zoological classification: family Felidae) are called felines and are divided into large felines and small felines, all of the genus *Felis*. A fundamental difference between big and small cats is that the latter are able to purr, but not to roar, while for the former the opposite is the case. The ability of large felines (including the lion, leopard, tiger etc.) to roar depends on a particular physical feature: at the base of the tongue is a piece of cartilage in the place of the hyoid bone, and this allows greater movement and thus the production of more sonorous sounds.

The first felids originated in the Eocene epoch, around fifty-four million years ago, but of these no fossils have remained. The earliest skulls available for study date from a later epoch, the Oligocene (about thirty-six million years ago). A distinctive feature of the felids of that period (considered primitive forms) was the exceptional development of the upper canine teeth which gave them the name of "saber-toothed" felines. The last primitive feline with saber teeth (genus *Smilodon*) became extinct about two million years ago, when the modern feline had already been in existence for a long time. In fact, the latter originated as a separate phylogenetic line from the common lineage during the Miocene epoch, about twenty-six million years ago. During successive epochs (from the Pliocene onward) characteristics emerged which differentiated the genera of modern felines.

The range of adaptability of modern felids has been very great, their geographical distribution extending to all the continents and larger islands, with the exception of Australia, Madagascar and the Antarctic. They have colonized every type of environment, from the desert to northern and tropical forests, as well as mountains.

By analyzing the physical structure and behaviour of felids it is possible to chart the main stages in their evolutionary history and in broad lines to trace this back to the environments they colonized. Their phys-

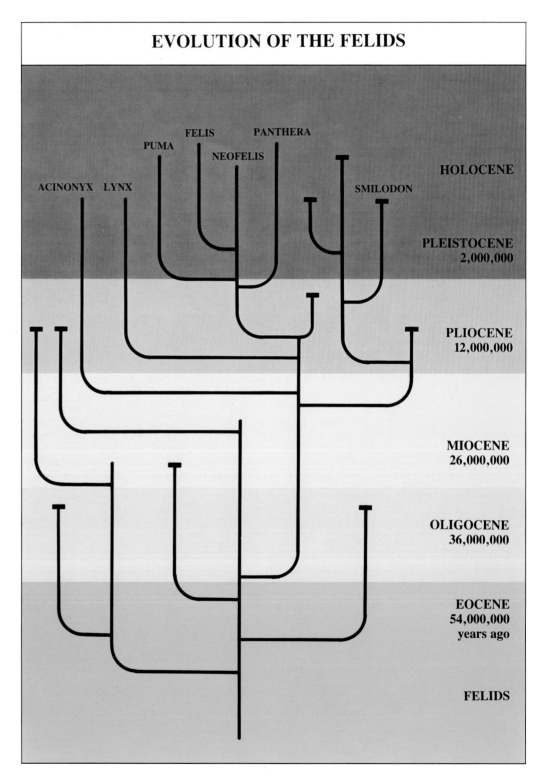

EVOLUTION OF THE FELIDS

ACINONYX LYNX PUMA FELIS NEOFELIS PANTHERA SMILODON

HOLOCENE

PLEISTOCENE
2,000,000

PLIOCENE
12,000,000

MIOCENE
26,000,000

OLIGOCENE
36,000,000

EOCENE
54,000,000
years ago

FELIDS

ical and behavioural adaptations proclaim the rôle of the predator, and felids are in fact among the most specialized of carnivores because they feed almost exclusively on meat, and almost always vertebrates. Although felines have the structure of predators, they are not built for speed: with the exception of the cheetah (*Acinonyx jubatus*), their hunting technique consists of the ambush rather than the long pursuit of their prey. Their bone structure allows them to make great leaps, and the structure of the forelegs enables them to strike out at their prey. The muzzle is short, not prominent, thus increasing the power of the jaw because the jaw bones, which act as levers, are also shorter.

The cat's retractile claws make it a great climber. Even those species that have colonized open or mixed environments such as the savannah, where tree climbing is no longer necessary for survival because they face no predator, apart from man, have retained this ability. In these environments certain factors, notably the large size of their prey, have been responsible for the remarkable increase in body dimensions, resulting in such great predatory machines as the lion or the leopard, (the lion = 270-365 lb/122-182 kg; the leopard = 66-155 lb/30-70 kg), which have the advantage of enormous strength combined with the agility of a small cat. In the forests, however, felids have not developed to an exceptionally large size, both because their prey is small (rodents, birds, reptiles, insects), and because their reduced size allows them better use of the refuges offered by the environment.

The small number of large felines (seven species) in comparison with the small felines (twenty-eight species), may be the result of their different rôle in the ecosystem. The former are large predators, feeding off other carnivores as well as herbivores, and constitute a significant energy cost to the ecosystem which is unable to support a large number of species. The latter, on the other hand, are intermediate links in the food chains: they are predators but, in their turn, are preyed upon by other

LARGE FELINES – (Seven species)	
Lion	*Panthera leo*
Tiger	*Panthera tigris*
Leopard	*Panthera pardus*
Jaguar	*Panthera onca*
Snow leopard	*Panthera uncia*
Clouded leopard	*Neofelis nebulosa*
Cheetah	*Acinonyx jubatus*

SMALL FELINES – (Twenty-eight species)	
African tiger cat	*Felis aurata*
Temminck's golden cat	*Felis temmincki*
Rothel's cat	*Felis badia*
Black-footed cat	*Felis nigripes*
Caracal lynx	*Felis caracal*
Fishing cat	*Felis viverrina*
Geoffroy's cat	*Felis geoffroyi*
Jaguarundi	*Felis yagouaroundi*
Jungle cat	*Felis chaus*
Kodkod	*Felis guigna*
Leopard cat	*Felis bengalensis*
Northern lynx	*Felis lynx*
Marbled cat	*Felis marmorata*
Pampas cat	*Felis colocolo* or *F. pacobita*
Ocelot	*Felis pardalis*
Pallas' cat	*Felis manul*
Pampas cat	*Felis payeros*
Puma	*Felis concolor*
Serval	*Felis serval*
Tiger cat	*Felis tigrinus*
European wildcat	*Felis silvestris*
Bobcat	*Felis rufus*
Chinese desert cat	*Felis bieti*
Rusty spotted cat	*Felis rubiginosus*
Sand cat	*Felis margarita*
Flat-headed cat	*Felis planiceps*
—	*Felis iriomotensis*
Margay cat	*Felis wiedi*

carnivores, and their energy cost is therefore less.

A particular characteristic of felids living in closed environments such as the forest is their extremely keen eyesight. In felines this appears to be the sharpest of the senses, more highly developed than smell and hearing. It has been proved that all felines, including the domestic cat, use sight as the dominant sensory system during hunting. The domestic cat can distinguish between different wave-lengths in the visual spectrum and, like most felines, has good night vision, thanks to its ability to dilate enormously the pupils of the eye, and thus detect objects and movements in the faintest light. Contrary to popular belief, felines cannot see in complete darkness, but in dim light their vision is up to six times more acute than that of humans. This indicates that they are twilight or nocturnal predators, but does not explain why such visual acuteness should have persisted in felines that inhabit a forest environment, where long-sightedness is not needed because of the lack of open spaces.

It has been proved that the *bullae osseae*, the part of the cat's skull connected to the hearing zone, are much more highly developed in felines that have settled in deserts and grassland than in those that have adapted to a forest environment, simply because acute hearing is less important in closed surroundings. It would be interesting to be able to measure the sight of felines living in the two different types of environment in order to establish whether there is a difference in sharpness of vision between them, but to date no such experiment has been possible. Because of this multitude of adaptations it is difficult to say with any accuracy what were the original surroundings of the main progenitors, from which the more modern genera of felids evolved. It is certainly easier to establish this fact in the case of the cheetah (*Acinonyx jubatus*), the most primitive of living cats, which developed as a separate species in the Miocene epoch. This was the same period of adaptation as for the members of the Artiodactyla (pigs, deer, sheep, rumi-

cecilia.'87   **Lion**

nants), excellent prey for big cats, and also the period in which the grasslands were formed. The cheetah is, in fact, the only runner among the felines, and is the fastest animal on earth, reaching speeds of 60 mph (96 km/h), although it cannot maintain such speed for long. It is the only member of the family with non-retractile claws, and it is not therefore suited to tree-climbing. To trace the path taken by the other felines is more difficult. For the *Panthera* genera an evolutionary sequence has been suggested that recognizes an early initial adaptation to hot, humid surroundings, and a gradual invasion of humid and cool environments by the tiger (*Panthera tigris*); tropical dry lands by the leopard (*Panthera pardus*), and equatorial dry regions by the lion (*Panthera leo*). But what of the remaining three species of large felines? These are the jaguar (*Panthera onca)*, which is found in a variety of environments, from tropical forests to marshes, deserts and savannah; the snow leopard or ounce (*Panthera uncia*), which is found in mountain steppes, and conifer forests; and the clouded leopard (*Neofelis nebulosa*), which has inhabited forests up to an altitude of 6,500 ft (2,000 m).

Of the history of the small felines, among which the lynx (*Felis lynx*), puma (*F. concolor*), ocelot (*F. pardalis*) and European wildcat (*F. silvestris*), very little is actually known. However, looking at all the members of the Felidae family, there is one common characteristic: the colour and markings of the coats. The tendency is for the coats to be yellowish, and the markings darker (almost always black), presented as spots or stripes, providing excellent camouflage while the animal is hunting or being hunted. In the lion the stripes have disappeared because the colour of the desert

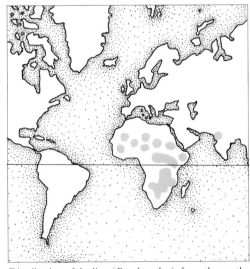

Distribution of the lion (*Panthera leo*): from the southern Sahara to South Africa, and in the Gir forest in eastern Asia.

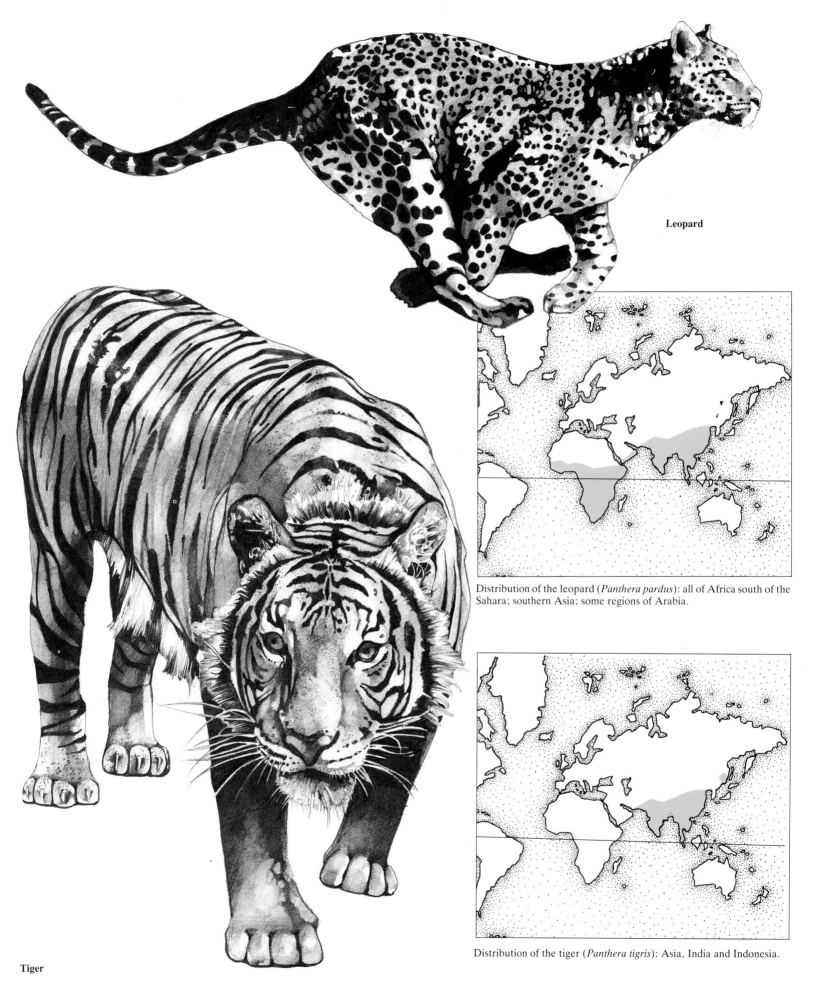

Leopard

Distribution of the leopard (*Panthera pardus*): all of Africa south of the Sahara; southern Asia; some regions of Arabia.

Distribution of the tiger (*Panthera tigris*): Asia, India and Indonesia.

Tiger

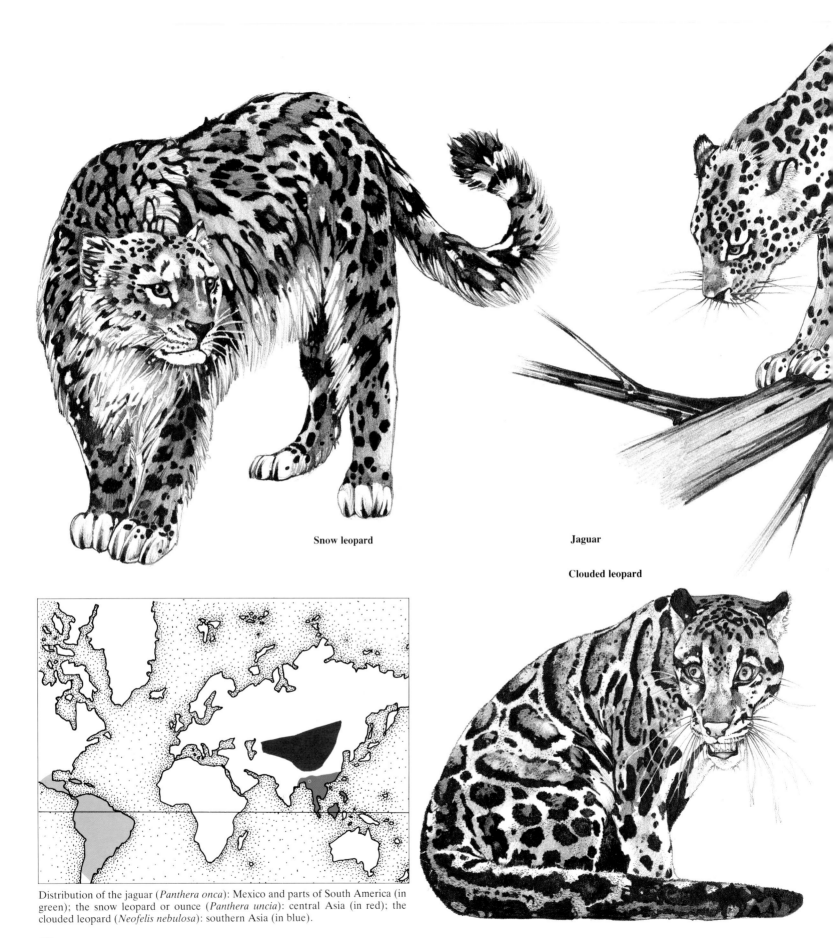

Snow leopard

Jaguar

Clouded leopard

Distribution of the jaguar (*Panthera onca*): Mexico and parts of South America (in green); the snow leopard or ounce (*Panthera uncia*): central Asia (in red); the clouded leopard (*Neofelis nebulosa*): southern Asia (in blue).

Distribution of the cheetah (*Acinonyx jubatus*): Africa and southwest Asia.

Cheetah

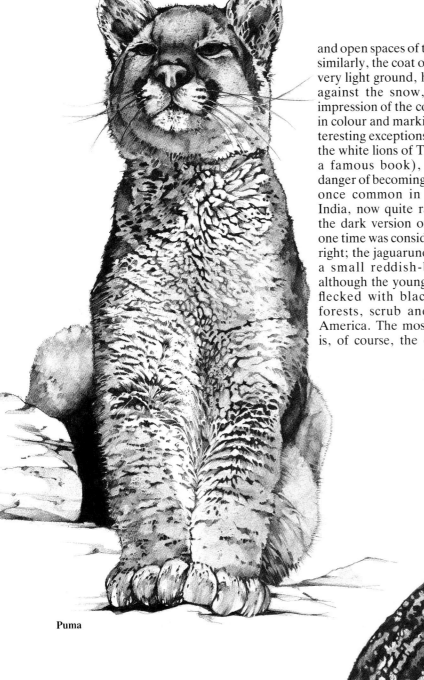

Puma

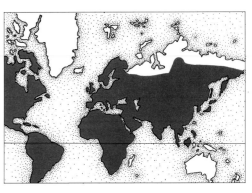

and open spaces of the savannah is uniform; similarly, the coat of the snow leopard has a very light ground, helping to camouflage it against the snow, although the overall impression of the coat is of uniformity both in colour and markings. There are a few interesting exceptions to this general pattern: the white lions of Timbavati (the subject of a famous book), which are albinos in danger of becoming extinct; the white tiger, once common in northern and central India, now quite rare; the black panther, the dark version of the leopard, which at one time was considered a species in its own right; the jaguarundi (*Felis yagouaroundi*), a small reddish-brown or grey felid, although the young are born with the coat flecked with black, which lives in the forests, scrub and grasslands of South America. The most notable of exceptions is, of course, the domestic cat, in whose coat the variety of colourings is remarkable. But the domestic cat is really the exception that proves the rule. Because it has abandoned its natural environment the variability of colour in its coat is no longer a disadvantage for the cat, whether as predator or as prey, and therefore has not been disfavoured by natural selection. It is not by chance, however, that the wild form of the domestic cat has a striped coat, very similar to that of the European wildcat (*Felis silvestris*).

Among the small felines the wildcat has been the subject of most research, with the aim, above all, of shedding light on the origins of the domestic cat.

Ocelot

The wildcat
(Felis silvestris)

The wildcat is thought to be the direct ancestor of the domestic cat in the sense that in one particular part of the world, or in several parts simultaneously, man probably domesticated a form of wildcat, identified as the species *Felis silvestris*. This cat still exists today: its distribution is wide, and includes Europe, Africa, and Asia.

This species presents three different "types" which do not co-exist in nature: the European wildcat, the African wildcat and the domestic cat. The classification of the three types has been the source of heated debate, and the controversy has not yet been resolved. Many scholars believe them to be representative of three different species: *Felis silvestris* (the European wildcat), *F. libyca* (the African wildcat), and *F. catus* (the domestic cat). This notion has been challenged in the light of experiments carried out on cats in captivity, in which

crosses between the various types produced lively and fertile offspring. Such results, however, do not exclude the possibility of the existence of three different species (in the wild there could be a pre-copulation barrier which does not operate in captivity), and have led to the proposition of considering them as a subspecies, and therefore calling them *F. silvestris silvestris, F. silvestris libyca* and *F. silvestris catus*. The question, however, remains open.

Another query is: which of the two wild forms was domesticated to produce the third, *F. catus* (or *F. silvestris catus*)? Certain facts have led us to suppose that the domestic cat is descended from *F. silvestris libyca* and not from *F. silvestris silvestris*. These include studies of skeletal remains (most importantly of the skull); the possible correlation between man's choice of habitat (mountain or grassland) during the period in which domestication is supposed to have

begun; morphological and behavioural adaptations encountered in the domestic cat (for example, a hearing apparatus suited to open spaces, and a specialized ability to capture prey, typical of grassland but not of the desert), together with discoveries of mummified Egyptian cats. Even this question has not been definitively resolved. Whichever is true, the fact remains that the domestic cat has enjoyed great success, colonizing all environments, and is found in all parts of the world inhabited by man. The same cannot be said for its progenitor, however, whether it be *F. libyca* or *F. silvestris*. Both are threatened with extinction because, unlike the domestic cat, whose evolutionary success is owed to its great ability to adapt, they are rather specialized, and adjust with difficulty to the drastic and sudden changes in the environment which typify the geographical areas inhabited by man. The main reasons for their decline are all linked with human interference, namely, the outright destruction caused through trapping, poisoning, and hunting, not to mention the breaking up, destruction and alteration of their habitat as a result of expansion in urban development, the construction of roads and motorways, and the exploitation of natural resources.

Knowledge of the wildcat's way of life and its chosen environment allows for interesting comparisons with the behaviour of the domestic cat, often shedding light on the significance of many of the latter's characteristics.

In the following analysis the wildcat will be considered without distinctions being made between its two forms, *silvestris* and *libyca*, since, in general terms, and for the purposes of this discussion, they present the same characteristics.

The wildcat's habitat consists of forest vegetation, and uneven rocky terrain, including valleys, gorges, hills and ridges, providing a variety of shelter for when the animal is resting, giving birth, and rearing its kittens: for this the female generally chooses well-hidden rocky outcrops, situated in remote woodland areas. Furthermore, the variety of the surroundings increases the variety of prey, another indispensable need for the survival of the feline. Studies of its predatory customs have shown that it feeds on a wide range of animals: mammals (rodents, rabbits, hare, etc.), birds, reptiles and insects.

Wildcats tend to be solitary. The only encounters between them are during the mating season, and while the female is on heat (five or six days on average). Gestation lasts about sixty-eight days, and there are usually three kittens per litter. The females generally have the first oestrus of the year – sometimes the only one – between January and February, which means that the kittens are born between March and April.

If the kittens of the first litter die prematurely, or if the female does not conceive after the first mating, she has a second period of heat, and produces another litter later in the year: for example, cases of wild-

Felis silvestris silvestris

cat births have been recorded in northern France as late as the end of October.

An interesting fact about the wildcat is that she gives birth straight on to the ground. Neither in captivity nor in the wild has the female ever been observed making a bed out of soft materials in which to give birth. Instead, she tends to scratch the earth to remove any dead leaves and other debris; similarly, when the domestic cat gives birth, she gets up occasionally, and, with her forepaws, scratches the bottom of the bed made for her by her owner.

The possibility has still not been excluded that the wild tomcat also has a period of oestrus. The question is debatable because it seems that in captivity males will mate at any time: in the wild, however, the male looks more actively for a sexual partner during the first months of the year. This could be due to the attractive and stimulating scent produced by the female, which will pervade the surrounding area during this period. The female rears her kittens with no help from the male: they separate at the end of the female's oestrus period, and do not meet again. In fact, she does not allow her young to come into contact with any male that roams into her territory, since the kittens could easily become his prey. Zoologists observing these cats in the wild have seen the male eat the kittens, but apparently this is not common. The young stay with the mother for three to four months, even though they are able to swallow solid food after thirty to forty days. It has also been observed that at fifty to sixty days old, kittens in the wild are able to avoid unarmed pursuit by humans, proving that they are perfectly aware and developed at that stage. After about five months they leave the mother.

Both males and females are sexually mature before they are a year old, even though their physical development is not complete until they are about two years old.

Wildcats are territorial animals. Their whole existence is conditioned by their tendency to take over and defend a clearly marked area within the environment in which they live, which then becomes their "protected area" or territory. This area usually provides its owner with food and shelter, and the cat will attack all outsiders, especially other cats, which overstep the boundaries it has marked with its special scent. In the animal kingdom, territory can be of different types: that of the individual, of couples, or of groups. With the wildcat the territory is individual (protected therefore against other cats of either sex), in the case of both adult males and females; rarely do territories belonging to individuals of the same sex overlap. Female cats are in fact much less tolerant of other females than males are of other males, a phenomenon probably due to their protective maternal instinct. The extent of the territory can be as great as 250 to 500 acres for males; some experts maintain that it is the same size for females, although, according to others it is half the size. The extent also varies during the year according to the availability of prey: when food is abundant, territories are smaller, and when it is scarce, they are considerably enlarged. The same happens when a female is rearing her young, since her needs increase. In all territories there is a central, totally exclusive area, providing various refuges in which the cat can sleep or lie in the sun, and – in the case of the female – in which she can give birth, and rear her young. The rest of the protected area is hunting territory, and overlapping may occur in these parts because here the "owners" are less aggressive. However, these are also the areas most strongly marked with the smells of the owner. The process of territorial marking involves the application of the animal's own odour to its surroundings. Wildcats make widespread use of this system, spraying urine (males more than females), depositing faeces, and also using secretions from cutaneous glands situated in various parts of the body, to mark their territory. When the cat excretes within its own territory, it buries its faeces; if, on the other hand, it wants to delimit the protected area, then it deposits its faeces along the boundaries. It has been noted, that cats deliberately choose conspicuous objects on which to

Felis silvestris libyca

"leave their mark," for example, on rocks and fallen trees. This brief description of the wildcat's habits is sufficient to show the extent to which its life is rigidly organized, and how this animal is bound by certain ecological necessities (the need for a variety of prey and refuges, its intolerance of encounters with man, etc.) to a particular environment.

It is very difficult to domesticate a wildcat, and impossible unless the animal is taken in in the first few months. Nevertheless man has succeeded in doing so. It is interesting not only to know how he achieved this, but also to consider why he should want to tame the cat as a domestic animal. If one were to observe an adult *Felis silvestris* the temptation to try the adventure would certainly not be great. In spite of their smallness (males weigh 6.6-17.6 lb/3-8 kg; females 4.4-11 lb/2-5 kg, with slight variations from one country to another), they are animals which inspire considerable fear by their aggressiveness. In spite of appearances, however, the fact that the wildcat must have some behavioural flexibility, is revealed by two phenomena. The first is the capacity of its direct descendant, the domestic cat, to live in social groups. This capacity is not found in the wildcat which, being an animal that preys on small creatures, cannot allow itself the luxury of sharing its food with others. The territory of a wildcat must therefore be exclusive if it contains sufficient prey for only one individual. The food resources of the domestic cat are completely different, and this has allowed the animal to organize itself socially.

The second phenomenon is connected with the very existence of the domestic cat: if there were not already present in the wildcat a certain behavioural flexibility predisposing the animal to domestication, the drawing together of man and cat may never have come about. This flexibility is seen, for example, in the inclusion in its diet, of food leftovers scavenged from houses or restaurants, and therefore very different from live prey. Let us now consider perhaps the most intriguing question: why did man want to take the cat into his home?

Theories on the domestication of the cat

The earliest date suggested for the beginning of domestication of the cat is 9,000 years ago, however, there are no fossil remains to support this theory. If, on the other hand, as certain experts maintain, the cat was first domesticated for the purpose of controling the rodent population, we must defer the event until at least 4000 B.C., since it was not until then that agrarian society had developed sufficiently for rats and mice to pose a serious problem, thus forcing man to introduce means of combatting them.

Although it is a known fact that the cat was domesticated in Ancient Egypt, since thousands of mummified cats testify to this, there is no such concrete evidence for other parts of the world where the same may have occurred; however, certain craniometric tests do support the hypothesis that the other most probable areas are central Asia and India, both ancient agricultural centers.

Knowledge of the date of domestication of an animal does not say much about the nature of its relationship with man: we should, in fact, consider that by domestication is meant the phenomenon of man rearing an animal, but in particular of his controlling its mating which, from that moment on is no longer subject to the process of natural selection, but to that imposed by man (artificial selection). To know when the effects of artificial selection on a living creature were first evident is only vaguely indicative of when the link between man and animal was forged. It may be for example that, for a long time, the wildcat lived side by side with man, without the latter interfering in its life. In support of this hypothesis, consider the case of the domestic dog *(Canis familiaris)*, the date of whose domestication has been established on the basis of fossil remains dating back 12,000 years. Two experts have recently found fossil remains in China which give grounds for supposing that there was a connection between a canine similar to the wolf, and Peking man as long as 500,000 years ago. Theories on domestication abound, but we shall limit ourselves for the purposes of this discussion to the most important.

Domestication for nutritional needs. In the past, cats have been used as a source of food, and are still eaten today in some parts of the world, the flesh of the wildcat being more highly regarded than that of the domestic cat. Clearly, if this is true today (although the animal is not now widely eaten), it must have been even more so in the past. It is unlikely, however, that man raised the cat originally as a source of food. Carnivores are generally not suitable for this purpose: their upkeep would cost the owner or producer too much, since it has to be fed on meat. In fact, the only carnivores that man eats today are fish, not mammals. Herbivores, on the contrary, represent a good investment, because their cost is modest in proportion to the quantity of meat obtained from them.

In conclusion, cats have never been widely used as food, although in times of war or famine they have provided a valid alternative to starvation.

Domestication for use in the hunt. This idea arose from the portrayal of the cat, depicted in the art of Ancient Egypt (3000 B.C.), in the act of aiding man during hunting. Clearly this has not been a very important rôle for the cat, and certainly not important enough to justify efforts to domesticate it. If this particular employment ever existed on a large scale, it must have soon fallen into disuse.

Domestication for the control of rodents. One of the most widely held theories for man's interest in the cat is linked to the animal's undeniable skill in catching rats and mice. Wildcats most likely moved closer to towns and villages because they were attracted by food refuse, and by the large populations of mice and rats which thrived in the ideal living conditions provided by human settlements. Having discovered the cat's skill at hunting, villagers encouraged the animals to stay close to their dwellings by providing food in limited quantities, and shelter. The link thus formed then developed into a greater bond between cat and man.

This leads directly to the last theory, which can be considered a complementary rôle rather than an alternative to that described above.

Domestication for companionship. Many experts agree that wildcats may have been domesticated simply to satisfy the natural tendency in man to take in wild animals with the intention of taming them. It may equally well have come about as a result of children's natural tendency to want to bring up the kittens of wildcats found in the countryside. The cat's domestication did not necessarily begin for utilitarian purposes. Another possibility is that the wildcat, which was allowed to live close to houses to hunt mice (but was not domesticated) gave birth to kittens which were taken in while still very small, and raised as domestic animals. It is clear that, at some time, over and above the utilitarian advantages that domestication of an animal could offer, man was tempted by the pleasure of having a member of a different species at his side. For centuries this social function has been developed with other animals, and so why not with the cat.

It is almost impossible to teach a cat tricks: reward or punishment rarely persuade it to perform actions against its will. It will show itself in public only for its own pleasure, or out of love for its owner. This is why it is rare to see stunts or displays in which cats are involved.

The cat today

T he heritage of the Middle Ages has, without question, been hard on the cat. In Europe the last official execution for witch-craft was in 1684, but for almost a further two centuries the cat was persecuted and tormented in every possible way. With the spread of education and the general improvement in welfare man has ceased to hound the cat and, at last, begun to take an interest in its qualities as a domestic animal.

This change in attitude was reinforced when, in 1871, Harrison Weir organized the first cat show at London's Crystal Palace. Since then cat shows have flourished, and having started as exhibitions staged by lovers of particularly beautiful or famous cats (for example, cats that had performed exceptional feats; or the largest cat ever seen; or representatives of breeds which were at one time very rare), they have de-veloped into promotional exhibitions for professional breeders, keen to show off to the public their extremely valuable speci-mens. But the rôle of the cat in modern society represents much more than a mere hobby or profession. The cat is often a partner in life for those who live alone; it also provides children with the opportunity of observing animal development and be-haviour, serving both an educational and emotional need.

Finally, the cat has a function, usually underestimated but by no means unimport-ant. The huge colonies of stray cats living in many cities owe their very existence to the devoted "guardians," who take care of them. The cats benefit directly, and are often fed regularly by individuals or groups of concerned cat lovers. The activity is mutually rewarding, and those who provide food for strays are frequently elderly people, for whom such a mission is an im-portant focal point in their routine, or people who for various reasons are not able to keep a cat of their own.

Last, but not least, the cat is still kept by many to carry out the job for which it has been prized since antiquity – that of rat catcher.

The cat
and genetics

Genetics should not be regarded as a boring abstruse subject reserved for those "in the trade." Indeed, in the case of the cat, a little knowledge of genetics can make the profession of breeder, as well as the amateur's hobby, far more interesting and enjoyable. It is more satisfying to follow the mating of two selected animals or, even, to anticipate what the colour of the coat or the eyes of kittens will be, rather than to continue by trial and error, probably puzzled, and misled by the results through sheer ignorance, and all because genetics is often considered too complex by the layman. This attitude has sometimes prevented the application of genetics by breeders of domestic animals, in spite of the fact that it frequently results in improvements to the breed (fewer numbers of animals used as "producers," improved strains in a shorter time, etc.).

The fundamental principles of modern genetics were discovered in a garden by the Austrian monk and botanist, Gregor Mendel (1822-1884). During his work as a teacher in the monastery at Brünn, he carried out experiments using garden peas (*Pisum sativa*). Mendel crossed seven plants that showed different characteristics of shape and colour of seed. He reached the basic conclusion that the appearance of the different traits followed specific laws, and that these laws could be determined simply by counting and recording the various kinds of pea produced by crossbreeding. In this way he demolished the theories of many biologists working at the time on hybridization using single subjects with varying characteristics, who believed that inheritance was a kind of cocktail, and the offspring essentially a "dilution" of the parents' differing characteristics. Mendel, in his simplicity, had a happy inspiration: after crossing "parents" with distinctly separate characteristics (yellow peas with green peas), he counted the number of yellow peas and the number of green ones obtained from each experiment. However high the number of experiments, the numerical results did not change. From

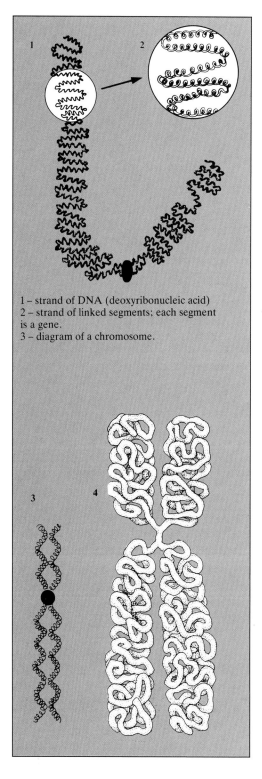

1 – strand of DNA (deoxyribonucleic acid)
2 – strand of linked segments; each segment is a gene.
3 – diagram of a chromosome.

each generation he obtained green and yellow peas in the same proportion. The inheritance did not "dilute" the characteristics; each one was transmitted without losing its identity, and corresponded to the laws of "all-or-none," either appearing in the offspring or, indeed, not appearing at all, or reappearing after several generations. The simplicity of this first step, which provided the answer to such a complex question, astounded the scientific world, especially as it became clear that the transmission of characteristics in other organisms obeyed the laws formulated by Mendel with the peas.

From peas to cats: however complex an organism is, its characteristics can be analyzed and identified because they correspond to Mendelian laws; it is therefore possible to act on them, and modify them with repeated crossings. This facility allows for the artificial selection by which man is able, for his own economic and aesthetic ends, to produce highly varied characteristics in plants and animals.

In genetics the factor responsible for transmitting the basic particulate unit of inheritance from one generation to another is called a gene. Genes are part of the DNA (deoxyribonucleic acid) chains which, with a complicated supporting structure of protein, form chromosomes contained in the cell nucleus.

Each chromosome is formed by a linear sequence of thousands of genes and can be visualized as a long string of DNA, like a string of beads. To put it simply, each gene, that is, each segment of DNA, corresponds to a particular characteristic of the individual, in this case the cat.

During cellular division each chromosome produces an identical copy of itself, and each daughter cell receives the same number of genes as the original cell. This duplication is very exact, and many thousands of duplications of a gene take place before an error occurs. These errors are called *mutations*. Mutations happen very rarely, and yet they are fundamental to the creation of variability; just consider that all the colours of the fur of the domestic cat are

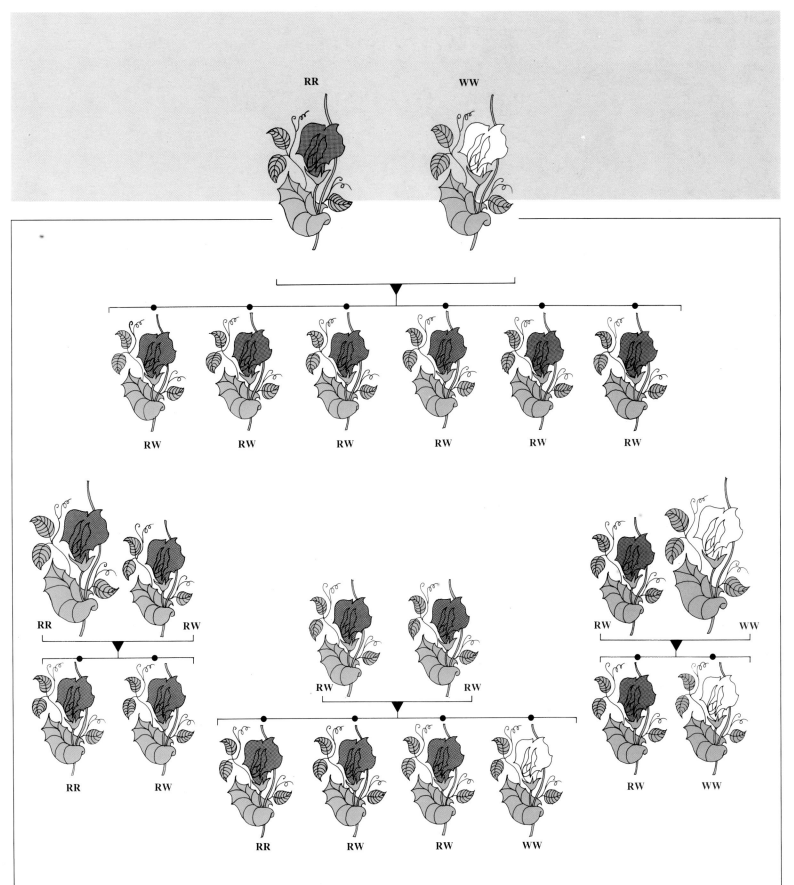

RR

WW

RW RW RW RW RW RW

RR RW

RW RW

RW WW

RR RW

RR RW RW WW

RW WW

Experiments on the inheritability of traits conducted by the Austrian monk Gregor Mendel on flowers of red and white peas. Starting with the crossing of two flowers, one with a pair of red genes and the other with a pair of white genes, a generation of flowers is obtained, the genes of which are red + white (even if they always appear red). If one of these is crossed with a flower with both genes red, the next gener-

ation will always be red but with 50% red + white genes and 50% red + red genes; if, on the other hand, a crossing is made with a white flower with white + white genes, the next generation will be red + white or white + white. If the crossing is made between two red + white, the next generation will be a 3:1 predominance of red over white. The genes will be 25% red + red, 50% red + white, and 25% white + white.

Mackerel Tabby

Self Black

owed to single mutations.

The cells of the cat contain thirty-eight chromosomes, each of which, in its turn, is made up of thousands of genes; the chromosomes are arranged in equal pairs, except for one pair of chromosomes in male cats, which will be discussed later. So, each cat possesses thirty-eight chromosomes, therefore nineteen pairs, two of each kind being homologous. Two "corresponding" genes occupying the same position (locus) on two chromosomes belonging to the same, homologous, pair of chromosomes are called *alleles*.

The alleles are either the same, in which case the individual is referred to as *homozygous*, for the characteristic coded by that gene, or different, and the individual is called *heterozygous*. In the more simple case, in which there is complete dominance, an allele is *dominant* (this is symbolized by a capital letter), or *recessive* (symbolized by a small letter). A dominant allele manifests itself whether it is present in two pairs, or in a single pair; the recessive allele, on the contrary, only manifests itself if it is present in two pairs because its effects are masked by the effects of the dominant gene if this is present. Thus the length of cats' fur is determined by a gene which pre-

sents itself in two allelic states. The dominant allele (L) causes the characteristic "short hair," while the recessive gene (l) causes "long hair." A shorthaired cat may therefore be either homozygous LL or heterozygous Ll, while a longhaired cat can only be homozygous ll. It is important to understand the distinction between the effect of a gene that is a phenotype or appearance, and the gene itself. The longhair gene, for instance, is a very small part of chromosome which shows itself in the development of an individual as the "longhair characteristic." In genetics the distinction is made for each individual between the genotype, that is, its genetic constitution, and the phenotype, which is the outward appearance of all its biological traits (colour, size, behaviour, etc.). The genotype is the genetic material the cat inherits from its progenitors: this remains relatively constant over time (the rare genetic changes are known as mutations).

The colours of cats' coats are a perfect illustration of the laws of heredity. All the different colourings of the coat are due to mutations from the original, or wild phenotype, the well-known striped coat of wild cats.

The wild phenotype is composed of two

colours: yellow-brown and black. In some parts of the coat the yellow-brown hairs predominate, in others the completely black. The yellow-brown colour makes up the background, carrying the black stripes and patches characteristic of striped and blotched cats. It is as if the black were a reticulation superimposed on the uniform, lighter background colour. It appears that one of the first mutations was due to an error in the duplication of the gene A (which causes a lighter background coloration) producing a new allele, a, which codes for full black. Cats with an aa genotype therefore, present this colour. This is how black cats were born. They were not the offspring of the devil and a witch, as was once widely believed.

If two pure tabby cats (genotype AA) are mated the resulting kittens will all be tabby. The same happens when breeding pure black cats (aa). If, however, a tabby (AA) is crossed with a black cat (aa), in the first filial generation (known as F_1) all the kittens are tabby. The tabby coat gene is therefore more dominant than the black coat gene, which is recessive. These tabby cats are therefore *hybrids* and also carry the recessive black gene, which shows itself only in the next generation. Crossing hybrids of the

F₁ generation produces a second, heterogenous generation (F₂) and, if the offspring is numerous, the ratio of tabby to black is in the region of 3:1. The blacks are all "pure-bred," like their black progenitors: mating between themselves produces always and only black cats, even in successive generations. The tabbies, on the other hand, are of two types: one-third are pure-bred, like the tabby grandparents, while two-thirds are hybrids, like the parents and, like them, they produce tabby and black offspring in the ratio of 3:1. Hybrids therefore produce kittens made up of 25% pure tabbies, 50% hybrid tabbies and 25% pure black (*the law of the segregation of characters*). Segregation is explained by the fact that heterozygotes produce gametes (the eggs of the female and the sperm of the male), which contain only one of the two alleles, *A* or *a*.

To understand this phenomenon a brief digression is necessary. We have already said that all the cells of an individual (for example, a cat) carry nineteen pairs of chromosomes, or thirty-eight single chromosomes. This is true for all the cells of the body except for the egg and the sperm cell. By a process called *meiosis*, the function of which is to prevent the doubling of the chromosome number in each generation, the gametes carry a single chromosome from each pair, so nineteen chromosomes in all. In the case of the tabby and black colours the gametes (sperm and eggs) will thus carry either the allele *A* (which produces the lighter background colour) or the allele *a* (which produces the black).

Table 1 below illustrates what happens in the mating of a pure tabby with a pure black: the tabby *AA* produces gametes that all carry the gene *A*; the black *aa* produces gametes all with the gene *a*.

In the first generation all the kittens will be heterozygous *Aa* and will be tabby because the *A* allele is dominant over the *a*. The black colour does not occur even if the allele *a* is present in all the genotypes.

How then can full black colour arise? Table 2 illustrates what happens when members of the first generation (F₁), all tabby but heterozygotes, are mated among themselves: each will produce not one, but two types of gamete, *A* and *a*, in equal numbers.

As we have seen, in the second generation (F₂) 75% of the kittens will be tabby and 25% black. This is in respect of the phe-

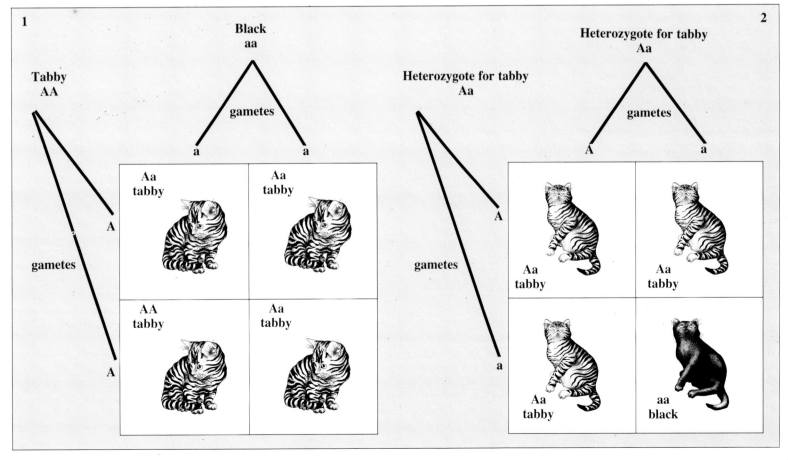

notype. As far as the genotype is concerned, 25% will be dominant homozygous tabbies (pure); 50% heterozygous (hybrids), carriers of the allele *a* for the colour black which, however, does not show itself because its action is masked by that of the allele *A*; and 25% will be homozygous recessive blacks (pure).

The naked eye cannot distinguish between the dominant homozygotes and the heterozygotes (consequently frequent use is made of the notation: capital letter-hyphen, for example L-, in which the capital denotes the dominant allele, while the second allele may be either dominant or recessive). This is what gives rise to surprises for the breeder who, convinced of having mated two of the purest champions, finds some unexpected colour in the litter. The numerical rule that determines the percentages of kittens of one type or another, if the genotypes of the parents are known, is the same as that formulated by Mendel for peas. However, we are not always dealing with cases of complete dominance; other cases will be illustrated in the descriptions of breeds when necessary.

This is a convenient point at which to state the two basic laws of Mendelian genetics, since these will appear clearer in the light of what has so far been discussed: 1) the principle of *segregation*, according to which the alleles present on a pair of chromosomes separate themselves during meiosis into two different sexual cells (gametes); 2) the law of *independence*, according to which the genes which segregate in the gamete behave independently of one another. For example, the gene responsible for a particular colour can be inherited independently from the gene responsible for long hair; in other words, their effects are not combined, and the traits are transmitted independently. Obviously there are exceptions to this second law, owing to the presence on the same chromosome of other genes coded for different characteristics. These characteristics tend to be transmitted together. It is not only coat colour and length of hair that have a genetic basis;

MALE SPERMATOZOA

	X	Y
X	XX female	XY male
X	XX female	XY male

FEMALE EGGS

many other characteristics, including size, shape of head, behaviour, etc., are also owed to the action of genes.

Finally, it is interesting to note that some characteristics have a particular action depending on the sex of the animal. They can show themselves in males, but be transmitted by females. This is the so-called "sex-linked heredity." The phenomenon is due to the fact that in the cat, as in many other organisms including man, there is a pair of chromosomes (the heterochromosomes or sex chromosomes), which differ in males and females. In the female this pair is formed of two identical chromosomes indicated as XX, while in the male there is one X chromosome, as in the female, together with a particular chromosome denoted as Y. All the eggs produced by a female will have one X chromosome while the spermatozoa produced by a male will carry half each of X and Y chromosomes. The sex of an individual is determined by the type of spermatozoa received from the father.

The genes on the Y chromosome will show themselves, obviously, only in males; those on the X chromosome will show themselves in males (which have a single X), whether they are dominant or recessive, because they are present in a single pair. In females (which have two X chromosomes) the genes are transmitted instead like those carried by the other chromosomes, for which a recessive allele shows itself only if it is homozygous. If the sperm which fertilizes the egg carries a Y chromosome, a male cat will result; if it is an X chromosome, a female, as shown in the chart on the left.

This brief introduction to genetics clearly disproves many popular beliefs: for example, when a cat which boasts a pedigree of championship in the show-ring manages to have a brief *affaire* with some unidentified street cat, the effects of this "illicit" love become evident in the litter. But there the trouble ends. Many people are convinced that the effects are long-term and that the "defiled" cat will no longer be able to produce pure litters, even if in the next heat she is mated with a pure champion. Nothing could be more wrong. We have seen that every kitten, produced from the union of an egg and a sperm, receives 50% of its mother's genes and 50% of its father's. Each conception is a new process, with new sperm; the cat cannot therefore be "defiled" by the previous mating because the sperm survive in the female genital tracts for a very limited time (a few days).

Glossary of genetic terms

Allele possible population of alternative forms of the gene which may occupy the same position on two chromosomes belonging to the same pair.

Chromosome any of several thread-like bodies, found in a cell nucleus that carry the genes, arranged in linear fashion; consists largely of DNA and protein.

DNA (deoxyribonucleic acid) – a long chain compound formed from many nucleotides bound together as a unit in the chain. A nucleotide is formed from one molecule of a sugar (ribose or deoxyribose), one molecule of phosphoric acid and one molecule of an amino group. DNA is found only in the chromosomes of plants and animals, and the corresponding structures in bacteria and viruses.

Dominant a gene is dominant to one of its alleles if it suppresses the phenotypic effect of that recessive allele when the two are together.

Gametes special cells known as sex cells that contain half the normal number of chromosomes. When a gamete unites with a gamete of the opposite sex during reproduction, the correct number of chromosomes is made up. In animals the male gamete is called spermatozoon and the female gamete, the ovum.

Gene a unit of heredity carried in a chromosome. A segment of DNA containing coded information which causes the appearance of a particular characteristic.

Genotype the genetic constitution of an organism at a particular locus or set of loci. In other words, the total number and kinds of genes encoded into DNA of a nucleus in each cell of an organism.

Heredity the genetic transmission of characteristics from one generation to generations of the same species.

Hetero-zygote an individual which has two different forms of a gene, the normal gene for a characteristic and its mutant, at the corresponding points on a pair of homologous chromosomes.

Homozygote an individual which has identical genes at corresponding points on a pair of homologous chromosomes. It will always replicate the same gene in its offspring.

Hybrid an individual obtained by crossing two individuals with different genotypes (for example, pairs, populations or species).

Locus a segment of a chromosome on which a gene is situated.

Mutation a spontaneous, localized change in the DNA of a chromosome, resulting in a possible difference in characteristics in individuals possessing it.

Phenotype the outwardly visible expression of a given genotype, that is, of the hereditary constitution of an organism.

Poly-morphism the presence in a population of more than one phenotypical form associated with alleles of one gene, or a group of genes.

Recessive describes a gene which only produces a trait, a quality, or a characteristic, when present with an identical gene (i.e. when homozygous for that gene).

Recombi-nation the occurrence in offspring of combinations of genes not present in either parent, caused by the random pairing of chromosomes and their associated genes during meiosis – a type of cellular division.

Subspecies groups of populations of a like species which are distinguishable by morphological characteristics, and sometimes for physiological and ethological characteristics.

Wild phenotype (wild type) phenotype of a species which is found in nature and can be considered as the original.

Genetics of feline breeds

Domestic cats are subdivided by breeders into various "breeds" on the basis of differences in general conformation, type, and colour of coat, etc. Before describing these differences in detail, let us examine the meaning of the word "breed" from a scientific point of view. In zoology "breed" (or subspecies) indicates a group of individuals which differ from others through a certain number of genetically determined characteristics. Notwithstanding these differences, individuals from different breeds mate normally and produce fertile offspring. The differentiation of the "true" breeds is the consequence of an evolutionary process which stems from the prolonged geographical isolation of population groups. For as long as they remain separate, such groups evolve independently of each other and, establishing different mutations, adapt to the particular environmental conditions in which they live. If this process of genetic differentiation is sufficiently protracted, breeds may evolve into different species. In this event, when groups reestablish contact, or when this is artificially

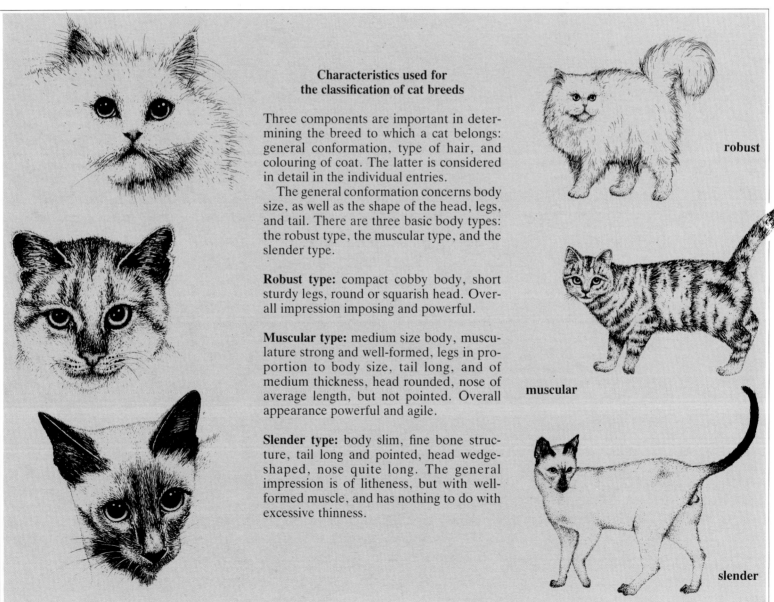

Characteristics used for the classification of cat breeds

Three components are important in determining the breed to which a cat belongs: general conformation, type of hair, and colouring of coat. The latter is considered in detail in the individual entries.

The general conformation concerns body size, as well as the shape of the head, legs, and tail. There are three basic body types: the robust type, the muscular type, and the slender type.

Robust type: compact cobby body, short sturdy legs, round or squarish head. Overall impression imposing and powerful.

Muscular type: medium size body, musculature strong and well-formed, legs in proportion to body size, tail long, and of medium thickness, head rounded, nose of average length, but not pointed. Overall appearance powerful and agile.

Slender type: body slim, fine bone structure, tail long and pointed, head wedge-shaped, nose quite long. The general impression is of litheness, but with well-formed muscle, and has nothing to do with excessive thinness.

robust

muscular

slender

arranged, they are no longer capable of interbreeding.

At the basis of the so-called feline breeds there are, obviously, processes of artificial selection (not natural). Moreover, as we shall discuss later, various feline breeds differ one from another by a single mutation (speaking exclusively of the colour of the coat); this is so, for example, in the case of the Abyssinian and the European tabby, but also of many others. From a strictly scientific viewpoint it is not possible to call them breeds, since genetically they are too close.

There is generally great confusion over the classification of coat colours, the proof being, paradoxically, that colourings that are the result of very disparate genetic combinations are placed together under a common denomination. Such is the case with the shorthaired self black and the self coloured white. At times these are the result of the action of genes (for example *aa* and *WW*) that have nothing in common. However, cats with these characteristics are taken as belonging to the same European shorthaired self colour breed.

This is true not only for traits in coats, but also for other physical characteristics. In order to be presented at cat shows, for example, Siamese cats must conform to certain standards: they must have slender, long bodies and well-proportioned wedge-shaped heads with triangular faces (to name but a few), while Persians, on the contrary, must be strongly built, the head quite large and square, and the nose shorter. But it is equally true that outside cat shows, all possible kinds of combinations can be seen,

---

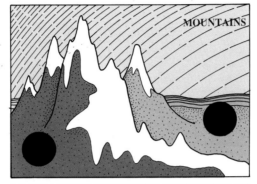

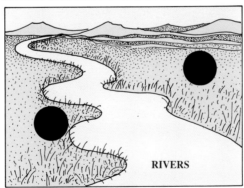

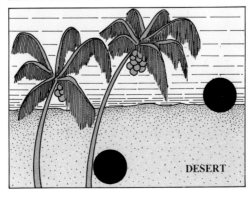

sometimes named one way, sometimes named differently. This is mainly due to two reasons: the first being the indiscriminate matings attempted in the home, in which selection of a particular characteristic of the coat is sought, with little or no attention paid to body structure; the second being the breeders who try to obtain new varieties (like the longhaired Siamese, that is the Balinese, which has neither the slenderness of the Siamese nor the robustness of the Persian), by combining characteristics of the coat with those of the body. This is why, ever more frequently, one sees a cat with all the appearances of a Siamese insofar as the coat is concerned (including the short hair), but with sturdy legs, round head and eyes, and a stocky body. The question is, then, to what breed should it be attributed? Most would describe it as Siamese, but experts would raise objections; in practice it can only be called a "Siamese not suitable for showing."

Bearing in mind that the genetic basis of bodily traits is complex and still practically unknown, let us now look at how the different phenotypes of cat have been categorized so far.

Each time that one individual appeared by chance in a litter, showing a mutation (for example, a longhaired kitten in a litter of Siamese, but with the same colouring as its brothers and sisters), breeders obtained numerous variants by crossing and recrossing the carriers of the mutation. When the result was eventually considered sufficiently individual and aesthetically pleasing, the decision would be taken to stop at that, and raise the animal to the category of a breed. Such was the case with the Siamese, the Burmese, and the Havana among others. Steps were therefore taken to ensure that cats carrying a particular character became homozygous for that character, in order that they remain pure.

By this criterion the shorthaired self white, and many others, ought to rise to the rank of breed (provided it is, for example, homozygous *WW*), as should the shorthaired, bicoloured black and white (always provided it is homozygous, dominant or recessive for that character). At the most there should be a breed for each coloration, recognized by international feline associations. If, on the other hand, account is taken of the above considerations, it would be necessary to abandon the habit of proclaiming as a new "breed" any and every variation on a theme. A Balinese is still a longhaired Siamese, and there are not enough genetic differences to make it a separate breed; while it is true that a Persian of whatever colour, is sufficiently removed genetically from a Siamese to be recognized as a different sub-group, even if a zoologist might not agree in describing them as two separate breeds.

What, then, is the solution? To try to eliminate the word "breed" from the common vocabulary would only cause problems because its use is far too widespread; however, to describe every pure coloration as a breed is incorrect. The term "breed" can perhaps continue to be used, but should be considered simply as a convention, useful because it is universally accepted. In other words, by convention one can speak of the Siamese, and the European tabby as belonging to different breeds, but at the same time one should bear in mind the reasons why they are not.

The coat of a cat consists of three different types of hair: 1 – guard hairs, which are quite long compared with the two others, and which taper toward the tip; 2 – bristle or awn hairs, which are thinner than the guard hairs, and thicken in diameter near the tip before tapering to a fine point. Together with the guard hairs these constitute the topcoat; 3 – down or wool hairs, which are known as the underfur or undercoat, are the finest of the three types, soft and downy. They are the same diameter from the base to the tip, and are undulated or "crimped."

The three kinds of hair have different functions. The first two protect the body against superficial knocks and blows, acting as a protective covering to the down hairs, and also serving a sensory purpose; the undercoat protects the animal from excessive heat loss. Differences between breeds

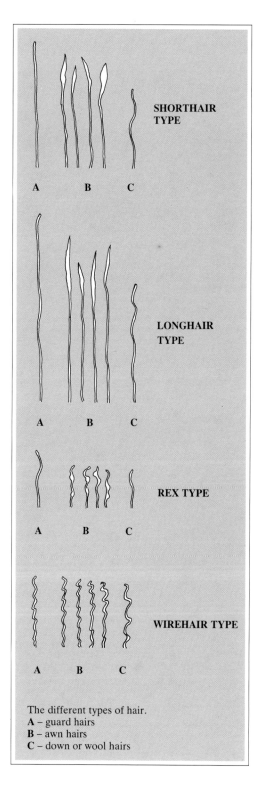

SHORTHAIR TYPE

A B C

LONGHAIR TYPE

A B C

REX TYPE

A B C

WIREHAIR TYPE

A B C

The different types of hair.
A – guard hairs
B – awn hairs
C – down or wool hairs

result from the modification of one or more layers of hair. The above description relates to the typical, compact and uniform coat of the shorthaired cat, which is determined by an *LL* genotype.

All shorthaired cats have at least one *L* allele. Persians with long, full, silky hair, possess instead the recessive mutant *l*, present as a homozygous pair. In these cats all three types of hair are present, but those of the guard hairs are exceptionally well-developed. Moreover, through the action of other modifying genes the underfur is also extremely soft and developed. The effect of these genes also shows itself in cats which are heterozygous *Ll*. These generally have hair of intermediate length, but not of the silkiness and softness of the Persian. It is not yet known whether the length of the hair is due to a faster growth rate, or to a normal growth rate, but over a longer period of time.

The case of the Rex, which has wavy hair, is completely different. At least three mutant genes have been identified, having presumably occurred independently, and are responsible for the growth of the "marcel-wave" type of hair. It is easy to think that Rex cats have only the third layer of hair, the soft wavy topcoat, but this is not exactly true.

All three types of hair are affected by the Rex mutants: the guard hairs and awn hairs are greatly affected and are either almost non-existent, or similar in length and shape to the down (only a microscopic examination can reveal the differences); the down hairs are almost normal, and are those most evident when the cat is observed with the naked eye. These anomalies are due to a slower growth rate in comparison with non-Rex cats. Let us look finally at the Wirehair: in 1966, in New York State two kittens were born with rough, curly hair, quite unlike the three layers of a smooth coat. It is now known that coarseness of this hair is due to an abnormal development of the usual three layers. The guard hair is softer than usual, the same length as the hair of the other layers, and curly rather than straight. The awn hairs deserve their name

colour, does not provide an absolute criterion for classification. For example, a European Calico, while having the same colouring as a Persian Calico, differs from it in general conformation and hair type.

To conclude this brief survey of cat breeds, and the genetic bases of the characteristics which distinguish them from one another, it is important to mention eye colour.

Rarely in other mammals is there the variety of colouring of the iris found in cats. Their eyes may be yellow or orange with all the intermediate tones, amber, gold, blue, green or emerald. Some of these colourings tend to be coupled with particular coats, giving rise to the belief that they are caused by the action of the same genes. The gene c^s, for example, which is responsible for the Siamese phenotype, probably also influences the blue colour of the eyes. It is significant that no Siamese has ever been obtained with green or amber eyes. Another gene that definitely affects eye colour is O which, as we shall see, determines the prevalence of orange over all the other colours of hair; it is probable that this gene also causes the tonal variations in the eye between yellow and orange.

But we can only suppose so much: the colour of the iris is almost certainly a polygenic character, and it is impossible to symbolize the genetic basis of the eyes with a single pair of alleles.

Genetic symbols should be regarded as a system of classification for showing what is, or is not, representable. Certainly, it is not yet possible to symbolize completely the interaction between genes.

We must therefore distinguish between characteristics more easily identifiable in the action of a gene (such as coat colour), and those for which it is impossible to attribute responsibility to a single gene (for example, eye colour or body type).

In the following section on the genetic bases of the principal types of coat and their variations we shall look at the genotypes with particular regard to the genes that determine coat colour and type, and to the mutants responsible for producing major changes in the coat colour.

of "beard," being exaggeratedly curved and coarse to the touch. The down hairs are also very curly. In fact the fur resembles the coat of a sheep rather than that of a cat. It would appear that this condition is inherited as a simple monogenic trait, as a dominant to normal coat, but further experiments are needed to confirm this hypothesis. The symbol proposed is Wh (for "Wirehair"). Many consider that this hair characteristic justifies the creation of a new breed, the American Wirehair, but the breed is still not recognized in Britain.

Only by the combination of the three components (general conformation, type and colour of hair) is it possible to establish the criteria for designating the breed of a cat. Even the third component, the hair

Genetic bases of the principal types of coat and their variations

EUROPEAN

Striped or Tabby. As we have already mentioned the tabby coat is believed to be the original coat, and has remained more or less unaltered to this day. Tabby cats are extremely common throughout the world, but are often the result of casual crosses, so that the precision of the black patterns on the yellowish-brown background is lost. The "pure" tabby coat must have well-defined black stripes, parallel to each other and with the fewest possible breaks; the tail must be ringed with black, and the head must have the mask of black stripes clearly outlined: typical is the letter "M" on the forehead. The lighter ground colour is yellowish-brown, referred to as *agouti* or ticked. This is sometimes enriched by a reddish shading (rufus modifiers) which recalls even more the coat of the wildcat.

The genotype of the wild tabby is A-B-C-D-T. Let us look at the pair of alleles that make it up: the lighter ground colour is caused by the presence of the A gene (for agouti), dominant in single or double pairs, indiscriminately AA or Aa. This colour, which is hard to describe because it is a mixture of grey, brown and yellow, is a result of the presence of bands of different colours in each hair. In the recessive homozygous condition (aa), one colour among those present in the bands of hairs prevails over the others.

A second gene, B (for "black"), contributes to the appearance of the black colour of the stripes. Its mutant, the allele b (recessive to B), is for "brown," and brings out a notable modification in the coat: black does not appear, and brown is seen in its place, as we shall see in the Havana Brown, which has chocolate pigment replacing the black.

Still in the dominant form, the C gene contributes to the full colour, with the gene D (for "dense") causing dense pigmentation. The recessive allele d, on the other hand, dilutes black to blue, and the tawny orange becomes cream.

The last dominant gene involved is the T gene (for "tabby"), which determines the vertical striping of the Mackerel Tabby. Its presence alone is not sufficient to produce the striped coat; the other genes mentioned are just as necessary. For example, if there were not a brownish-yellow ground colour, the black stripes would not stand out. Furthermore, the lack of the dominant A gene in black cats causes a defect which prevents them from competing in cat shows. Everyone must have seen a cat which at first sight appeared uniform black but, in a different light, showed reddish with indistinct markings. This type of animal probably has the pair of alleles T- and, at the same time, the recessive pair aa, responsible for uniform black. The result is evanescent stripes, described as a "ghost pattern" because, depending on the light, "now you see them, now you don't."

In the genotype of cats with a tabby coat, however, the four genes involved all present at least one dominant allele, and that can be considered as an earlier primordial state. Mutations of these genes have led to a series of colorations very common in our cats.

The first mutation to consider is that regarding the T gene, which has contributed to the success of the phenotype presented at cat shows as the Blotched Tabby, both the shorthaired and, as we shall see later, the longhaired varieties.

The genotype for the Blotched Tabby is A-B-D-t^b t^b, differing from the Mackerel Tabby by having the t^b allele. Since t^b is recessive to T it must be present on both loci of the allele (i.e. homozygous genotype $t^b t^b$) for the blotched phenotype to appear (a genotype Tt^b would again produce a tabby phenotype). The markings on the head are similar to those of the striped cat, but the pattern on the body is quite different. Instead of being straight, the black bands form circles and spirals, and the legs and tail are ringed. The ground colour is still agouti, similar to the striped cat.

There are many variations on the blotched coats because, having been chosen as the standard for presentation at cat shows, artificial selection was focussed on them. Indeed, while only a few striped variations exist, produced more by chance than design (the Red Striped, or the Silver Striped), there is a far greater number of blotched coat colours, for example blue, lilac, chocolate, orange.

It is interesting to note that, theoretically, it is possible to obtain any variety of striped coat already obtained for a blotched coat, given that the two phenotypes differ in only one pair of alleles: T- for mackerel striped; $t^b t^b$ for blotched.

The genotype of the Silver Tabby is worth noting, since it demonstrates that Mendel's laws of complete dominance do not always hold. The genotype of the Silver Tabby (A-B-I-T) possesses the gene I (for "inhibitor"), which suppresses the deposit of pigment in the hair during growth, the result being white hairs with coloured tips. This gives a silver colouring to the coat, seen to great effect in the Chinchilla Longhair. Since the I gene's action asserts itself only on certain other genes (gene T, responsible for the striped coat is not among them), the result is a cat with a silver, rather than an agouti (ticked) base coat, striped normally with black. The same applies to the silver blotched coat (genotype: A-B-I-$t^b t^b$).

In blue blotched tabbies gene D is replaced by the recessive d, which must be present on both loci of the allele: A-B-$dd t^b t^b$. The effect of the recessive gene d will be analyzed in detail for the self or solid-colour blue coat (Korat, Russian Blue and Chartreux). The stripes are slate-blue and the ground a delicate cream or fawn. The Brown Tabby (genotype: A-$bb D$-$t^b t^b$) shows bands of a rich chocolate colour against a yellowish ticked ground. The characteristic of this genotype is to have the gene b recessive to B (see Havana Foreign; U.S.A., Havana Brown).

The self colour which completes the series is the lilac (genotype: A-$bb dd t^b t^b$). Here, both gene b and gene d are evident (see Havana Foreign, Korat, Russian Blue and Chartreux), and it has a genotype not

very different from the Blue Blotched Tabby. The ground colour is lilac-fawn, that is, dilute brown, with striping of a darker tone. For further information on the striped cats, see the Egyptian Mau.

Selfs. All self (solid-coloured) cats are non-agouti in that they must have the pair of aa alleles. If, in addition, they were to possess a single A gene, the colour of the hairs would not be uniform, but banded. The first variations concern the four usual colours: the original (in this case, black, derived from mutations of the tabby), blue, chocolate and lilac. To take the black cat first: it must not have even the smallest of white markings. Its genotype is $aaB\text{-}D\text{-}$, in which aa produces the non-agouti colouring (that is, the hairs are not banded), the pair $B\text{-}$ produces the shading in the black (unlike its mutant b, which produces the less intense shading of chocolate; see Havana Foreign), the pair $D\text{-}$ produces the density of the colour black (compare the Korat, the Russian Blue and the Chartreux). The coat should be free from any brownish markings.

The genotypical and phenotypical characteristics of the full blue will be dealt with in the paragraph on the Korat, Russian Blue and Chartreux.

The Self Chocolate has been regarded

from the beginning as a breed in its own right, known as the Havana.

The lilac variety of coat (genotype $aabbdd$) is particularly rare and attractive. It is, in fact, a lighter and more delicate shade of blue, as if it were a diluted blue. The process that leads to its appearance can be described as the black coat undergoing two transitions: to the pair of recessive genes aa is added the homozygous recessive pair bb, which represent the first transition from black to brown. The presence also of the homozygous recessive pair dd causes the coat to undergo a second dilution from brown to lilac. Having three pairs of recessive alleles, the lilac cat is by definition

pure, because the colour could not occur if all three pairs of alleles were not present in homozygous recessive form. It is to this that its rarity is due.

Completely white cats occur through the action of the gene symbolized by W (for "white"). Since this is dominant, even the heterozygous Ww will be uniformly white. This does not signify a complete lack of pigmentation, as in the case of the albino with red eyes (see Siamese): the white is due to the action of the W gene which masks the effects of the other colour-producing genes. Most white cats are heterozygous Ww, probably as a result of repeated crosses attempted by breeders for various reasons,

perhaps to obtain orange eyes. The *W* gene does in fact affect eye colour. When the cat is homozygous dominant *WW*, the eyes are generally blue. Sometimes the gene causes a side-effect, so that some white cats with blue eyes may be deaf. This is not always the case, but the phenomenon is sufficiently recurrent for it not to be considered accidental. White cats have also been obtained with eyes of different colours (one blue, one orange).

The white coat resulting from the *W* gene should not be confused with the white coat produced by the *S* gene (see Bicoloureds, even if the two are phenotypically indistinguishable.

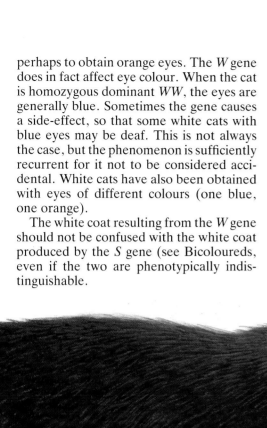

European Self Black

51

European Orange

Eighteen pairs of homologous chromosomes and one pair of sex chromosomes (heterochromosomes). The latter determine whether an individual is male or female, as demonstrated in the chart below. The male possesses one X and one Y chromosome, while the female has a pair of chromosomes XX. The chromosomes are arranged in descending order of length, and are grouped according to their particular morphological characteristics. Then they have been divided into groups (indicated by the capital letters), within which the individual pairs are numbered. The pair of sex chromosomes is considered separately.

Orange. This colour is transmitted in a particular way in that it is sex-linked; in other words, it is located on the X chromosome. The orange colour is due to a physiological alteration of the pigments of the hair, which is determined by the *O* gene; two alleles are known, *O* and *o*. In the case of a homozygote *OO*, the typical tabby coat (agouti ground with superimposed black stripes) will show as an orange tabby, and the black cat will show as uniformly orange. The heterozygote *Oo* will present with orange and black patches, known as tortoiseshell. In this case there is codominance, in other words, both the alleles show in the heterozygote.

Only the heterozygote *Oo* will produce a cat with a tortoiseshell coat because some areas of the coat are affected by *O*, and are orange (ginger), and others by *o* and are black. Since the males have a single X chromosome they can have either a single *O* gene, in which case they will be ginger or orange, or a single *o* gene, in which case they will be black. But the females, having two X chromosomes can have the genotype *OO* (orange phenotype), *Oo* (tortoiseshell phenotype) or *oo* (non-orange phenotype). Only a female can have tortoiseshell colouring, while a male will be either all orange or all black. There are, in fact, very rare cases of tortoiseshell males with two X chromosomes plus a Y. The Y would produce male characteristics, and if one of the X chromosomes carries the *O* gene and the other *o*, the result would be an XXY male – of genotype *Oo* – a tortoiseshell. Such males are usually sterile. It is therefore impossible to obtain a "pure" tortoiseshell breeding line. They can originate only from the crosses illustrated in the diagram on the right.

Taking into consideration the other genes which control coat colour, the female orange tabby has the genotype *A-D-OOT-*, while the male is *A-D-OT-*; the female self orange or ginger is *aaD-00* and the male *aaD-O*. Gene *B* is not included in this description of genotypes because, due to the presence of *O* it has no effect on the phenotype, neither in the dominant nor in the recessive form.

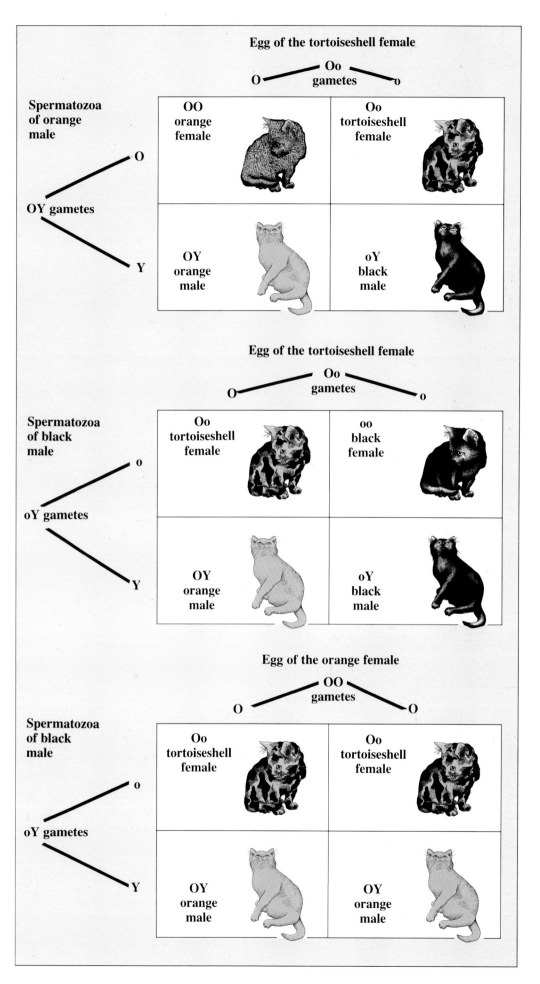

European Cream

European
Tortoiseshell

Bicoloureds. Cats presenting two colours are very common. One of the two colours is always white, the other often black, but may be blue or chocolate. The white areas are due to the gene S (for "piebald"), which has the effect in certain parts of the coat, of eliminating the pigment-producing cells. The results are very variable, as is the size of the affected areas; they first appear on the belly, then on the neck and chin, and may extend to include the forelegs and chest. The gene S seems to be inherited as a dominant, in that cats without white markings produce offspring also without white markings, while parents patched with white hairs produce offspring patched with white. The degree of marking can vary from one extreme to the other, represented by a completely black cat (genotype aaB-D-ss), and by a completely white cat (genotype aaB-

D-SS). All bicoloured white and blue coats will be aaB-$ddSs$, while the white and chocolate coats will be $aabbD$-Ss.

Calico and **Cream.** The calico coat is patched with white, orange (ginger) and black. The genotype will be $aaOoS$-. The white colour is due to the pair of alleles S-. It has been noted that the more white is present, the larger are the patches of a single colour. As yet there is no explanation for this phenomenon, but it may be due to the greater or lesser effect of the S- gene.

The cream coat and the blue-cream are diluted varieties of the Red Tabby and the Tortoiseshell respectively. The colour is diluted by the presence of d (for "dilute") in the genotype. The male cream has ddO incorporated into the genotype; the cream female, $ddOO$. A blue-cream (female) will be $aaddOo$.

SIAMESE

The colour of the Siamese cat is owed to a gene (c^s) which is one of a series of different mutants of the same gene. The wild type C (for "full colour"), which determines a uniform coloration, is dominant to all the other mutants. The second is the allele c^b (responsible for the coloration of the Burmese cat). The third is the gene c^s, responsible for the characteristics of the Siamese. It should be noted that c^b is recessive to C and dominant to c^s. Two other mutants in the series are the c^a, which produce an albino cat, devoid of pigment, and with eyes that are either blue or of no colour; and c, which gives the name to the whole series known as the "albino series" since it produces cats with no pigment, and pink eyes. It is recessive to any other element in the series.

A cat can, of course, have only two alleles from the series, one per chromosome, therefore it could have either $c^s c^s$, or $c^s c^b$, but never $c^s c^s c^b$.

The Siamese genotype is non-agouti (that is, like the Self Black) with the addition of the homozygous pair of genes $c^s c^s$. Thus it will be aaB-$c^s c^s D$-. It is therefore impossible to identify the place of origin of the Siamese insofar as it could have originated anywhere, through mutations in a black cat.

The increased density of colour toward the distal parts (extremities) of the body seems to be due to the different temperatures of the various parts of the body. Where the temperature is lower (in the case of warm-blooded animals this would be at the extremities) the coat is darker compared with the rest of the body. This behaviour of pigment shows of course only if in the genotype (of an individual) the gene c^s or c^b, is present.

The variations from the typical Siamese, obtained by appropriate crossings, also show this phenomenon by which, whatever the shade of colour of the coat, the extremities are darker. The varieties obtained are: Siamese Blue Point (aaB-$c^s c^s dd$); Siamese Chocolate Point ($aabbc^s c^s D$-); Siamese Lilac (frost) Point ($aabbc^s c^s dd$); Seal Tabby (lynx) Point (A-B-$c^s c^s D$-) which, in effect, is a variety of the Tabby since it has the dominant form of A instead of its recessive mutant a. Finally, by using individuals carrying the O gene (responsible for the colour orange), the following have been obtained: the Siamese Red Point ($aac^s c^s D$-O for the male; $aac^s c^s D$-OO for the female), and the Siamese Cream Point ($aac^s c^s ddO$ for the male; $aac^s c^s ddOO$ for the female).

It is quite safe to assume that by continuing to experiment with genotypes, and by trying different and new combinations, other types of Siamese can be obtained.

KORAT
RUSSIAN BLUE
CHARTREUX

The basic genotype is aaB-dd. This means that the gene for uniform black, a, must be present as a homozygous pair aa (the condition of having identical alleles at a chromosomal locus), the colour is therefore non-agouti, as all the selfs, but the colour is lighter than black through the presence of the gene d. This allele is a mutant of the D gene, and is inherited as a recessive; to express itself, it must therefore be present on both loci of the allele. A black cat has black pigment uniformly distributed in each hair, so that the coat is of solid colouring, devoid of shading. In the blue cat on the other hand, because of the gene d, the pigment (which is in fact black) is distributed irregularly along the hair, and under microscopic examination is seen to be deficient in some parts of the hair, and concentrated in others. This gives the coat its different shadings of grey, and the incidence of the light plays its part in determining the opalescent effect. The pigment is irregularly distributed along each individual hair, and for this reason the result is not a blotched cat, as in the case of the tortoiseshell, but a cat with varying shades, since each hair is individually affected by the play of light and shade. By way of analogy, the effect of the coloration produced by the gene d is similar to the impression created when a field of corn is stirred by the wind: the ears of corn rising and falling in continual movement give the impression of an extent of colour that is uniform, but with a thousand nuances. The d gene also shows the colour orange, which becomes cream. The effect on the coat is the same, whether cream or blue.

HAVANA
FOREIGN

In the section on selfs or solid-colour coats the third variant, the Self Chocolate, has been left in abeyance. The genotype is, of course, non-agouti (aa) like all other unicoloureds, so that the individual hairs will be of one colour, and not banded with different colours. There are two mutants that produce uniform brown in place of black: b and b^l. These represent two different shades of brown, one dark, the other light. Both cause the formation of brown pigment instead of black.

The genotype of the Havana Foreign is $aab^l b^l D$- for the lighter shade, which is distinctly paler and shows a ghost tabby pattern under a bright light: for the darker shade the genotype is $aabbD$-. The pair of alleles aa determines the single colour (not banded) of the hairs, the pair bb the formation of brown pigment, and not black; in the case of the pair $b^l b^l$ the pigment subsequently becomes lighter. The pair D- causes the pigment to be uniform along the length of each hair, giving the appearance of full colour and not of diluted colour as in the blue or cream coats.

EGYPTIAN
MAU

It is still not known whether the phenotype of the Egyptian Mau is determined by a specific gene or whether it is a modification of the European Tabby. It is currently indicated by A-B-D-T, the symbols used to indicate the genotype of the wild European Tabby (without the gene C), and therefore incorrect for the ordinary Egyptian Mau – a somewhat confusing situation. Clearly, there must be some other genetic factor which causes the stripes not to be continuous, and the coat to be spotted, but it has not yet been identified. The same holds for the Blue Mau (A-B-ddT-), the Bronze

Mau (which is the Chocolate Tabby: A-bb-D-T-), the Lilac Mau which appears in two shades: light (A-b^lb^lddT-), and dark (A-$bbddT$-), the Cinnamon Mau (A-b^lb^lD-T-), and the Silver Mau (A-B-D-I-T-). All these genotypes are purely indicative, and do not explain the differences with the corresponding varieties of European Tabby.

ABYSSINIAN

Abyssinians have the agouti gene A. The coat is composed of banded hairs, the pattern where present showing only minimal traces of a darker shade than the base colour. The peculiar characteristics of the coat are determined by a mutant of the gene T: the T^a allele. This is why books on genetics include it with the tabbies. Its genotype is A-B-D-T^a, which means that it has the same genotypical characteristics as the European Tabby, except for the pair T^a.

The mutant T^a appears to be dominant over the original allele T. As yet, however, the genetic constitution of the Abyssinian is not completely clear. Different varieties have been produced, all splendid: the Blue Abyssinian (A-B-ddT^a-) has a cream ground colour and bluish ticking; the Chocolate Abyssinian (A-bbD-T^a-) is very much darker than the ordinary brown, with abundant darker brown ticking all over the body, and a deep chocolate tail tip; the Lilac Abyssinian (A-$bbddT^a$-) has lilac ticking over a cream ground.

Problems have arisen over the definition of the Red Abyssinian, the most sought-after and best-known variety. The difficulty stems from the fact that the expected colour does not correspond to a definite genotype, because the ground colour is uniformly agouti, to which are added the effects of certain genes which produce unexpected results. The Red Tabby is produced by the sex-linked gene O, but the colour of the Red Abyssinian is inherited as a simple recessive to normal. The Red Abyssinian of genotype A-b^lb^lD-T^a- is actually the Cinnamon Abyssinian, although it appears to have red ground colour with brownish striping. The genetically Red Abyssinian has the genotype A-B-D-OT^a- (male) and A-B-D-OOT^a- (female). The colour in this case is more brilliant with orange-red ticking. There is also confusion over derivatives of the red genotype, such as the cream, tortoiseshell and others. It is therefore as well to bear in mind that in the Abyssinian there is a discrepancy between genotypical constitution and phenotype, a confusion made worse by the fact that many different varieties of coat have been produced, such as the Cream Abyssinian, the Tortoiseshell Abyssinian, and many varieties of the varieties (Chocolate and Cinnamon Tortoiseshells, etc.).

The Silver Abyssinian deserves special mention. The gene responsible for this coat colour is the inhibitor I: this inhibits the appearance of agouti, giving a silvered effect, while not inhibiting the development of pigment in the ticking. Its genotype is A-B-D-I-T^a-.

BURMESE

Let us look again at the question of the albino series of alleles described in the section on the Siamese. This is made up of C (self colour, black and orange or red), c^b (Burmese), c^s (Siamese), c^a (albino with blue eyes), and c (albino with pink eyes). The gene c^b causes the formation of dark sepia-coloured pigment in the place of black, and yellow in the place of red or orange. The typical Brown Burmese has the genotype aaB-c^bc^bD-. The Blue Burmese has of course the pair dd (aaB-c^bc^bdd), the Chocolate the pair bb ($aabbc^bc^bD$-), and the Lilac all the homozygous recessives ($aabbc^bc^bdd$). The blue coat is a bluish-grey, the chocolate, a warm light brown colour, the lilac a greyish-pink "dove" shade. In the United States the chocolate is called "champagne" and the lilac "platinum." There is also the Red Burmese, aaB-c^bc^bD-O (male), and aaB-c^bc^bD-OO (female), with a fine golden-red coat. Finally, there is the Cream Burmese, aaB-c^bc^bddO (male), and aaB-c^bc^bdd-OO

(female); the Tortoiseshell Burmese, *aaB-c^{b}c^{b}D-Oo*, and the Blue-Cream, *aaB-c^{b}c^{b}ddOo*; the Chocolate Tortoiseshell, *aabbc^{b}c^{b}D-Oo*, and the Lilac Tortoiseshell, *aabbc^{b}c^{b}ddOo*. In the United States there is a variety of coat similar to the Burmese known as "Tonkinese." Genetically this cat is a Burmese-Siamese (*aaB-c^{b}c^{s}D-*) being heterozygous through the *c^b* and *c^s* alleles of the albino series, and may be described as the light-phase Burmese, or the dark-phase Siamese. The colour differences between the body and the extremities are more accentuated than in the Burmese. The eyes are blue-green.

REX

The Rex genes still require a great deal of investigation. At the moment there are considered to be three independent Rex genes: *r, re, ro*, but only two breeds are recognized by cat associations or societies: the Cornish Rex and the Devon Rex. Here, as with the Scottish Fold and the Manx, it is not colour that is the distinctive characteristic of the breed, but the type of hair, which must always be curly. A Blue Devon Rex will have the genotype *aaB-ddrere*, while a Tortoiseshell Cornish Rex (female, of course) will be *aaD-Oorr*; a White Cornish Rex will be *rrW-*, a Cream Devon Rex will be *aaddOOrere* (female), and *aaddOrere* (male), and so on. In the description of the genotypes of tortoiseshell and white coats certain genes are excluded because in the presence, respectively, of *O* and *W*, their effect is not felt.

The curly coat is inherited independently of the colour of the coat. Both the Cornish and the Devons have only one thick curly coat with almost no guard hairs, and no undercoat. Matings between Cornish and Devons are undesirable in the context of keeping the two breeds pure, and also because not enough is yet known of the

interaction between these genes. Separately, it seems that they may be recessive to normal straight hair, but crosses between themselves give unexpected results. The few crosses effected have produced kittens showing the characteristics of both breeds (thick fur which gradually becomes more sparse because individual hairs break, with curly or broken whiskers).

Attempts have been made to produce a longhaired Rex by crossing Persians with Cornish Rexes. The result has been a cat of the genotype *llrr* (*l* is responsible for the long hair) with curly fur longer than normal, but not as long as that of the Persian.

PERSIAN

Self colour Persians can be black, blue, chocolate, lilac, white, red or cream. The ensuing genotypes, and the action of the various genes involved have already been dealt with in detail in the section on European Selfs (black, lilac, white), European Orange (red, cream), the Korat, Russian Blue and Chartreux (blue) and the Havana (chocolate).

Black: genotype *aaB-D-ll*. The colour must be completely devoid of reddish tints (avoid lengthy exposure to the sun), of lighter-coloured hairs, and of markings. Eyes: yellow or orange.

Blue: genotype *aaB-ddll*. A phenotype which has undergone artificial selection more than any other. The shadings must be various tones of grey or blue, never reddish or yellow. Striping excluded. Eyes must be brilliant orange or copper-coloured.

Chocolate: genotype *aabbD-ll*. The same colour as the Havana Foreign. Must be uniform. Eyes copper-coloured.

Lilac: genotype *aabbddll*. The general impression is of a pinkish-grey, like a dove. Eyes light orange or copper.

White: genotype *W-ll*. The eyes must be orange, blue (in which case the cat will probably be deaf), or odd, that is, one eye blue, the other orange. The coat colour must be pure white without shading or even a touch of cream. Needs a lot of care because of a tendency to turn yellow. Has nothing to do with the albino coat which is devoid of pigment. When heterozygous (*Ww*) it may carry the gene *w* for the pigment, which will appear in the offspring of the next mating (*Ww* × *Ww*).

Red: typically this genotype is non-agouti like all the selfs, which means that it contains the homozygous recessive pair *aa*. So the male is *aaD-Oll*, and the female *aaD-OOll*. Occasionally, however, Red Persians, genotypically Tabby, are included in the categories of Persian Selfs because the length of the hairs causes them to overlap, disguising the coat pattern. Even though, theoretically, this should not happen, they are frequently accepted as Selfs with some coat pattern. The eyes are copper-coloured.

Cream: genotype *aaddOOll* (female) and *aaddOll* (male). The eyes are copper-coloured.

Tabby: the Persian or Longhaired Brown Tabby has the same genotype as the European Striped Tabby, plus the pair *ll*. As with the European, it is more rare than the Blotched Persian. The Brown Tabby has the genotype *A-B-D-llT-*. The other striped tabbies have the same genotype as the blotched which will be the examples given as they are the more frequent, with the pair T- in the place of $t^b t^b$. The Brown Tabby (blotched): genotype A-B-D-$llt^b t^b$; Red Tabby: (female) D-$llOOt^b t^b$ and (male) D-$llOt^b t^b$; Blotched Silver: B-I-$llt^b t^b$; Blotched Cream: dd-$llOOt^b t^t$ (female) and $ddllOt^b t^b$ (male).

The Tortoiseshell (aaD-$llOoss$) and the Calico (tortoiseshell and white, aaD-$llOoS$-) can only be female (see European Orange).

The Blue-Cream Persian derives from the Tortoiseshell Persian through the colour dilution exerted by the recessive alleles dd. The genotype is therefore $aaddllOo$. Eye colour is the same as for Europeans of equivalent coats.

Bicoloureds. All Persian bicoloureds are subject to the effect of the S gene (see European bicoloureds for greater detail). There are numerous colour combinations, but one of the two colours is always white. The white markings are not extensive but usually cover the legs, the lower part of the body, the chest and the face. The most frequent combination is black-and-white (aaB-D-llS-); blue-and-white: (aaB-$ddllS$-); red-and-white: D-$OllS$- (male) and D-$OOllS$- (female); cream-and-white: $ddOllS$- (male), and $ddOOllS$- (female). The eyes are always copper-coloured.

Chinchilla, Smoke and **Cameo.** In the genotype of all three the inhibiting I gene causes the absence of pigment (see European Silver Tabby), so that the colour is present only in the tips of the hairs. The coat, whatever the colour, becomes lighter as the hair grows longer, the pronounced white undercolour shows and the pattern disappears, only the extreme tips of some hairs being pigmented. It is as though there is a shadow on the surface of the coat which deepens or lightens if the cat is stroked. This is how it happens: in passing your hand over the back of the cat, from head to tail, the fur is flattened and the cat appears darker; if you pass your hand in the opposite direction the

shadow disappears because the white undercolour is uncovered. The Chinchilla appears to be tinted with silver because it has white hairs with black tips. Its genotype is A-B-D-I-ll. The eyes are blue-green or emerald.

The Smoke Persian also shows the effect of the I gene, each hair being uniform dark grey as far as the tip. It is rare for the undercolour to be white; often it is grey of varying shades. So, both the Chinchilla and the Smoke are "silvered," although the Chinchilla is generally the lighter in colour.

The kittens of both varieties show vague traces of tabby pattern at birth, either blotched or classic. This usually disappears in the adult, although in some cases it may remain. To give but a brief explanation of this phenomenon, suffice it to say that it is linked to the common origins of the Smoke, the Chinchilla and the Silver Tabby Persian. The basic genotype of the Smoke Persian is aaB-D-I-ll, but other varieties have been produced which reveal shading of different colours: grey-blue (aaB-ddI-ll); grey-chocolate ($aabbD$-I-ll); grey-lilac ($aabbddI$-ll). The eyes are orange.

The Cameo or Red Smoke closely follows the same pattern: it is the result of bringing together the genes I and O. The hairs are therefore pale orange or cream at the base and red at the tips. There are three intensities of shading: the lightest, Shell Cameo, shows an almost white fur with rather indistinct reddish tinting; the second, Shaded Cameo has a warmer, more intense colour at the tips of the hairs; and the most heavily shaded, Smoke Cameo, has dense veiling, rendering the lighter undercoat almost invisible. The genotype of the three coats is D-I-llO (male), and D-I-$llOO$ (female). A cream variety has been produced with the genotype ddI-llO for the male, and ddI-$llOO$ for the female.

The Tortoiseshell Cameo has a light undercoat, and hair tipped with tortoiseshell, as if brushed with black, red and cream spots. The genotype is D-I-$llOo$ if the darker parts are smoke, or D-I-$llOo$ if the darker parts are silvered, as in the Chinchilla. In other words, the first is derived

from the heterozygous pair Oo on the coat of the Smoke Persian, the second from the action of the same pair Oo on the Chinchilla coat. The diluted tortoiseshell varieties with cream in the place of red, and blue instead of black are, respectively, ddI-$llOo$, and ddI-$llOo$. The eyes of all Persian Cameos are a warm copper colour.

COLOURPOINT

The genotype is the same as that of the Siamese, plus the homozygous recessive pair ll. The genotype for the seal is aaB-$c^s c^s D$-ll. Variations are: blue (aaB-$c^s c^s ddll$); chocolate ($aabbc^s c^s D$-ll); lilac ($aabbc^s c^s ddll$); red female ($aac^s c^s D$-$llOO$), and red male ($aac^s c^s D$-llO); cream female ($aac^s c^s$-$ddllOO$) and cream male ($aac^s c^s ddllO$); tortoiseshell ($aac^s c^s D$-$llOo$) and blue-cream ($aac^s c^s ddllOo$). The breed is known as the Himalayan in the United States.

SOMALI

The Somali differs from the Abyssinian by the presence of the homozygous recessive pair ll. Thus, the genotype is A-B-D-llT^a-. The long hair is not, however, full and silky like that of the Persian, probably because the Somali lacks the other modifying genes for the development of the hair, which would give it extra length.

Two colours are known: the normal Ruddy type, the genetic base of which is given above, and the Red Somali (A-$b^l b^l D$-llT^a-). As in the case of the Abyssinian there is a discrepancy between the genotypical constitution, and the colour actually obtained. The red colour is not, in fact, due to the action of O (absent in the genotype described), but to other phenomena, discussed in the section on the Abyssinian.

Cameo Persian

Shorthaired breeds

European Shorthair

British and
American Shorthairs

There are many varieties of the common European cat: striped, self, blotched, spotted and others. On the basis of what we have already discussed on the concept of breed, many other types, themselves described as breeds, could be included in this group, among which: the Bombay, the Exotic Shorthair, the Ocicat, and the Oriental Shorthair (names which are not always indicative of their place of origin). With this, one is, in fact, saying that the types of cat mentioned have many common genetic characteristics and that, for example, the slanting eyes of the Oriental Shorthair (which the others do not have) are not enough for it to be considered a separate breed in its own right.

The aim of this book is not to attempt to solve the thorny question of the nomenclature of feline breeds, but rather to explain the theories on the origins of certain characteristics of our cats, leaving to authorized feline societies the task of establishing the criteria for distinguishing one breed from another. The hypotheses on the domestic cat's origins have already been discussed: it would seem to be descended from the African Wildcat (*Felis silvestris libyca*). The cats that lived with the ancient Egyptians, and the cats that spread from Africa throughout Europe, by way of the Greeks and Romans during the flowering of their respective civilizations, as well as through European populations during the Middle Ages, are all considered to be descendants of *Felis silvestris libyca*, and all are shorthaired. Pictorial evidence up to the year 1500 confirms this; it was not until after 1500 that cats of other colours began to appear.

Great Britain was the first country to establish a "breed" for shorthaired cats, including even alternative colorations of the mackerel striped and blotched (or classic) patterns, no longer considering tabbies mongrels. This breed was called the British Shorthair, although in many other countries it was grouped together with the European Shorthair.

Silver Tabby, classic pattern

Silver Tabby, mackerel striped

The name "tabby" comes, in fact, from Iraq. Al'attabiya was a quarter of Baghdad where silk was manufactured; the weavers reproduced the colours and designs of cats' coats on these silks which were then sent to Europe, and sold under the name tabby.

American Shorthairs are generally considered to be descended from British and European Shorthairs. Slightly larger and more athletic than their European counterparts, the American Shorthair is bred in a full range of coat colours and patterns.

To conclude, a breed does exist with well defined, genetically transmitted traits, and which, in this text, is called the European Shorthair. This breed includes all short-haired domestic cats with the following characteristics: cobby, quite powerful body; wedge-shaped or round head, but not flattened like the Persian; large ears set well apart; eyes of varying colour depending on the coat, but without gradations of other colours (for example, yellow eyes must not be speckled with green), round in shape or

slightly almond; tail not too thick, but pointed. These features briefly describe the "common cat," in which refined physical extremes, such as the flattened face and robustness of the Persian, or the pointed nose and slenderness of the Siamese, do not figure.

The character of the European Shorthair can vary greatly since historically it is the product of many crosses. One particular trait is assured, however: it is an extremely intelligent animal.

European Cream

Siamese Red

SIAMESE

The Siamese is one of the most famous types of cat because the standards set for the breed were established around the 1880s, and it has therefore spread much more widely than other breeds. The differentiation of the domestic cat into various breeds was deemed necessary, in fact, in honour of the Siamese and Persians, which were the only cats different from the "common cat" presented at the first cat shows at the end of the nineteenth century.

The popularity of the Siamese is owed to its distinctive coat, which is light on the body with darker tones on the extremities (face, ears, paws, and tail). The name, as with the Persian, is vaguely indicative of its probable area of origin, which seems to have been Asiatic. Its introduction into Europe came toward the end of the nineteenth century. It is claimed that Siamese cats were exhibited at the London Cat Show in 1871, although other sources maintain that the first two pairs (Pho and Mia, Tiam O'Schian and Suzan) were brought to London by the English consul, Owen Gould, in 1884, on his return from Bangkok in Siam (as Thailand was then called, which would account for the name of the breed). It reached the United States soon after. The colours of their coats immediately attracted the public's attention; demand for these cats was so great that, in their attempt to satisfy it, breeders carried out too many matings between closely related pairs, and consequently soon weakened the breed. The physical characteristics of the first Siamese were slightly different from those

Siamese Lilac Point

Chocolate Siamese

of today: they were in fact more cobby and less elegant. Moreover, they frequently presented a slight squint which is today considered a defect. There is a charming legend attached to the kinked or curly tail which sometimes appears in Siamese cats. It is said that the Princesses of Siam welcomed such a feature in their cats because they used them as a place of safekeeping for their rings.

Legends having had their day, the general aspect of the breed conforms to precise criteria. Siamese cats must be sin-

uous, very slim, and graceful. The head must be markedly wedge-shaped, and the nose pointed. The ears must also be pointed, the eyes bright blue (no other colour is permitted), almond-shaped and inclined towards the nose, in typical oriental style. The long tail should end in a point. Contrary to popular opinion, and still believed by some today, the kinked or curly (corkscrew in fact) tail are not valuable and distinctive characteristics of the breed, and should be avoided. In actual fact, characteristics of the Siamese are practically the

exact opposite of those of the Persian. To risk a general statement, the same can also be said for character: Siamese cats are extremely lively, exuberant, and capable of great displays of affection. Liveliness of character also means that they have a tendency to run about, over furniture and up curtains and, on the whole, they are fairly intrusive. Their voice is particularly harsh and penetrating. However, they are interesting animals, with all their contradictions, but never as mischievous as many cartoon animators portray them.

Blue Siamese

KORAT
RUSSIAN BLUE
CHARTREUX

Although showing differences in other physical characteristics, these three cats have been grouped together because they have the same genotype as far as the genes which control the coloration of the coat are concerned. Unfortunately the genetic basis of such characteristics as bodily dimen-

Korat

72

Korat

sions, shape of the head, and colour of the eyes, is complicated and still not clear. In all three cats the coat is full blue, that is, a colour which varies from light grey to dark grey with dark shading. The colouring also extends to the skin. Some maintain that the three breeds show differences in the shade of blue, and the subject continues to be a cause for debate.

The Korat is of medium size. Its head is similar in shape to that of the Tabby, in other words quite rounded, with a tapering but not pointed muzzle. The ears, of medium size, are set apart and rounded at the tips. The eyes are green. The Korat has played an important part in the folklore of its country of origin. It originated in the province of Korat in Thailand where it is still called Si-sawat, and is believed to bring good luck. It arrived in the United States in 1959 but was not officially recognized as a breed until 1966 in America, and 1972 in Europe. From a scientific point of view, it is of interest that, by comparison with ancient portrayals of cats, the Korat still looks exactly like its ancestors.

The Russian Blue is also known as the Russo-American Blue, or the Maltese Cat, although it came from neither America nor Malta and, perhaps, not even from Russia. It is thought to have been imported into England on board a merchant ship from Russia. However that may be, it is certainly popular in Britain.

The Russian Blue is a graceful, slender cat with long lines. The head is quite wide; the eyes must be yellow without speckling, or green. Its character is similar to that of the European Shorthair with which it is often confused.

The Chartreux is certainly more clearly differentiated than the Korat and the

Russian Blue

Russian Blue. It is popular in France, and represents the continental version of the Russian Blue. Among the theories concerning its origins the most reliable revolves around a cat reared by Carthusian monks in a Charterhouse near Paris. It is a rather old cat, mentioned in Buffon's *Histoire naturelle* of the thirteenth century. It is stocky and muscular; the head large and the muzzle rounded (but not flattened), vaguely resembling the conformation of the Persian. The eyes are amber-yellow or orange. Its character is rather reserved, it is not intrusive and does not often mew.

Its colour is full blue, and this coloration (with the same genotype *aaB-dd*) can be found in the European Self Blue, in the Scottish Fold (which, however, has ears folded forward), in Manx cats (tailless), and in the Persian, although in this case the fur is long. In all of these instances, in accordance with Mendel's second law, distinctive characteristics of a breed (the folded ears, the lack of tail, long hair, etc.) are transmitted independently of the colour of the coat. In conclusion, then, the colour blue can be produced in many breeds, regardless of other characteristics.

Chestnut Brown

HAVANA

Havana Brown
Chestnut Brown

This dark brown cat is recognized as a distinct breed in its own right by international cat associations, and goes by the name of Havana. It is a Self Chocolate cat, a later case of a breed which differed from another (from the Self Black, for example) by a single mutation.

The Havana coat must be a solid colour all over the body. The skin is pink, as are the pads of the paws. The body is slim with fine bones, but muscular. The back legs are slightly higher than the front. The head is not too large, longer than it is wide, and the muzzle is slightly pointed. Its green eyes are oval-shaped. The ears are striking, wide-set and pointed.

The history of the Havana does not date far back, since the breed was not officially established until 1956. Referred to as the Havana Brown in the States, and the Chestnut Brown in Britain, it is a cat of distinguished bearing, reserved in its displays of affection.

78

Havana Brown

EGYPTIAN MAU

This is the only domesticated form of the spotted cat. In fact it would be quite difficult to single it out from the many cats in the streets that have been left to interbreed freely, and that once presented a coat that was originally mackerel striped, but now have broken stripes resembling small spots.

The Egyptian Mau is distinguished by the capital letter "M" on its forehead, and the typical mask of the European mackerel striped tabby, as well as the ringed tail and striped legs. On closer examination, what distinguishes it from the common cat is that the spots are more or less regular and evenly distributed.

The Mau's body is slim, lithe, graceful and well-proportioned. The head is small and wedge-shaped, the ears large and wide at the base. The eyes are green, yellow or hazel, almond-shaped but not slanting.

Like the Siamese, the Abyssinian and all slim, well-formed cats, the Egyptian Mau fascinates by the elegance of its movements. It is an intelligent, friendly, and affectionate animal.

In ancient Egyptian "Mau" meant "cat." The modern Egyptian Mau has been given this name because it is considered to be the cat that most closely resembles the cat of Ancient Egypt, at least judging from tomb paintings, and other artistic remains of that age. The Mau was bred in the United States in the early 1950s from cats brought from Egypt, in an attempt perhaps, to return to the original, or at least to one of the first cats domesticated by man.

Bronze Egyptian Mau

ABYSSINIAN

At first glance the Abyssinian gives the appearance of a self coloured cat. But on looking through any text on genetics one may be surprised to find it included among the tabbies. Examine the Abyssinians more closely, and faint traces of tabby pattern will be apparent, almost a "ghost" pattern, on the head, limbs, tail, and, more faintly, on the chest. They make the Abyssinian unique among cats: their bodies are uniform in colour while the head and tail are faintly marked.

The Abyssinian is a splendid animal, agile, slender, and extremely elegant. Its legs are long, its bearing graceful. The head is small and wedge-shaped with large, rounded ears; its almond-shaped eyes are green, yellow or hazel.

The cat arrived in England around 1860, imported from Abyssinia, and was officially recognized as a breed in 1929. The Abyssinian does not like close confinement. It is lively and athletic, and therefore not suited to living in an apartment where it does not have access to a garden. It is a prolific animal. The Abyssinian is very affectionate, and loves attention. It has one very odd trait: it loves water.

BURMESE

The Burmese is another cat which, in times past, was venerated as a divinity. Legend has it that it came from Burmese monasteries. It is actually portrayed together with other cats, in a book of poetry from the Ayudhya period (1350-1767) from Thailand (formerly Siam). Modern genetics have revealed that the Burmese is closely related to the Siamese, from which it differs in its more compact muscular body, and broad chest. The head is not quite as long as the Siamese; in fact, it is shorter, with large ears rounded at the tips. The golden yellow eyes are almond-shaped. The points are darker than the body colour and it would seem that this phenomenon, as with the Siamese, results from variations of temperature in different parts of the body. The darker colouring of the points is less evident in adults than in kittens.

Its character has some traits in common with the Siamese, which is to be expected: it is highly inquisitive, lively and rarely frightened by anything unfamiliar. Its voice is strong, although not quite as harsh and penetrating as that of the Siamese.

86

MANX

The existence of this breed, together with the Japanese Bobtail, the Sphynx, and the Scottish Fold, is the irrefutable proof of man's exploitation for his own ends of biological phenomena, even of genes which cause more or less serious deformations in animals, and which should, in theory, be eliminated. In cats a long list of such genes exists, some of them lethal, meaning that they cause the death of the embryo before birth, or the death of the individual before the start of the reproductive period. Others simply produce gross deformities. Cases have been recorded of polydactyly (extra toes on the forepaws), diseases of the retina, malformation of the legs and the palate, more than two ears, total lack of the tail, and so on. Breeders have selected three or four of these malformations which they find visually attractive, and have elevated them to the status of distinctive characteristics of a breed. In the case of the Isle of Man, the anomaly determined by the *M* gene (for "Manx") may express itself in four different ways: total lack of a tail sometimes with a small hollow where the vertebrae would normally issue; an immovable

tail stump felt as an upright projection, consisting of a very small number of tail vertebrae: this type is known as the "rumpy-riser"; a mobile tail stump with a slightly longer tail, usually deformed; and the fourth type, which is the most rare, is the "longie," consisting of a tail that is longer than any of the others, but shorter than normal. However, only the total absence of the tail is acceptable in show cats. In these specimens the vertebrae themselves are missing. The *M* gene has various effects, generally negative: it sometimes provokes malformation of the spinal column by reducing the length of certain vertebrae, causing them to fuse. Malformation may appear in the sacral and pelvic bones. There may also be problems in the formation of the anal opening, causing bowel stoppage, which will become evident when the kittens begin to take solid food.

The breed known as Manx includes carefully selected individuals which become valuable specimens. At the same time it must be remembered that their principle characteristic, the absence of a tail, is determined by a gene which is lethal when homozygous (there are in fact no *MM* individuals because they are still-born). In heterozygous individuals (*Mm*) there can be side-effects. The results of mating two heterozygotes is shown in the diagram below. The homozygous dominant *MM* dies in the uterus during pregnancy and is reabsorbed.

All colours of coat are allowed: Manx cats may be tabby, self coloured, bicoloured, or tortoiseshell. The body structure is similar to that of the European Shorthair, with the single difference (apart from the lack of a tail) that the hind legs are invariably longer than the forelegs, giving the Manx a hopping gait like a rabbit.

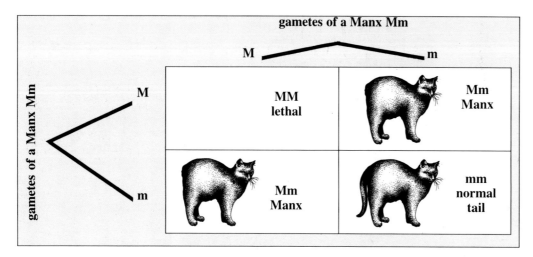

90

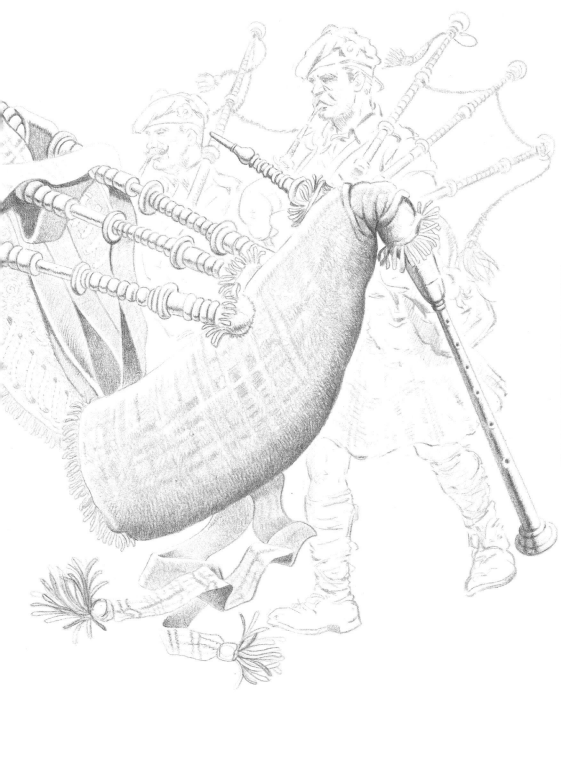

SCOTTISH FOLD

One of the anomalies of genetically determined development is represented by this cat's ears, which are folded forward and downward. The kittens are born with normal ears but at about four weeks of age, instead of continuing to grow upright into the "pricked" position, the ears tend to fold forward. This tends to give the cat a very appealing, almost startled expression. Other characteristics add to its resemblance to a toy: the head is completely round, the eyes are also very round, wide open, and staring. The body is cobby with sturdy legs and a thick tail.

The accepted coat colours are the same as for the European Shorthair: any colour and pattern are allowed, but the colour of the eyes must harmonize with that of the coat.

The folded ears are inherited as an incomplete dominant (symbol Fd). This cat is usually heterozygous ($Fdfd$); the homozygote $FdFd$ causes a defect in the development of an endocrine gland, the epiphysis, which produces abnormally short, thick tails, and swollen feet, causing great difficulty in walking. The heterozygotes do not produce these problems. If you become the owner of a Scottish Fold, it will probably be a heterozygote. It is as well to mate it with an ordinary cat, as 50% of the offspring will be Scottish Fold, in their turn heterozygotes, and so spared any of the above problems.

REX

The body conformation of the Devon is similar to that of the Siamese, and is markedly slender. The Cornish is also slender and muscular; both breeds have long legs and thin tapering tails. The head is triangular and the nose should have a strongly marked stop, the forehead curving back to a flat skull. The eyes are round and the colour should harmonize with that of the coat. The ears are large. The Rex has a calm disposition, and is well-suited to apartment life.

Rex cats are characterized by short, wavy or curly hair. Cats of this type have been reported in many different parts of the world, and it is presumed that the determining mutations have occurred independently. The first known Rex cat was born in 1950 in Cornwall, England, in a litter from two normal shorthaired cats. It gave rise to the breed known as the Cornish Rex; the gene involved was symbolized by r. In 1960 another case was reported in Devon, England. This breed was called the Devon Rex and the symbol chosen for the mutant was re.

In 1951 a cat with wavy hair was born in Germany. The phenotype was called German Rex but no name was assigned to the gene because, after various breeding experiments, it was considered to be identical to r. Finally in 1959, a cat with the fur typical of the Rex was born in Oregon in the United States. The symbol proposed for the mutant was ro and the breed was named the Oregon Rex. Strangely, if an Oregon is mated with a Cornish or Devon Rex the kittens have normal straight hair.

The Cornish and Devon Rexes differ from each other in some characteristics, chiefly in the composition of the coat. The Cornish seems to lack the primary guard hairs but has a denser coat. The Devon has awn and guard hairs (neither breed has underfur) but a thinner coat, and is prone to have bare areas. The brittle awn hairs are thinner than the guard hairs and break easily, even by the cat licking them. As the cat spends a large part of its day washing itself, a tendency which becomes instinctive after the first month of life, it is understandable that the Devon Rex shows sparse fur with patches of skin evident, especially on the stomach, which lasts until the next moult. Selective breeding should be able to rectify this. The whiskers of the Devon Rex are little more than stumps and it appears (although there is no certainty) that they break off as the animal grows. The whiskers of the Cornish Rex are shorter than normal, sometimes bent, but do not seem to break.

Cornish Rex

Devon Rex

Calico Bobtail

Black Bobtail

JAPANESE BOBTAIL

Little is known about the genetic factor which causes the formation of the Bobtail's very short, often curved and rigid tail. It would seem, however, to be connected with the *M* gene of the Manx cat. Malformation of the skeleton, or of other organs have not been encountered, so whatever the genetic basis for the stumpy tail there could be no specific physical reason for it.

The Bobtail is a lithe, slim cat with a fairly long, triangular head and large ears.

The eyes are oval and their colour must harmonize with the coat; in the case of tricoloureds the eyes must be yellow. Theoretically, coat colour can be of any type, but breeders are progressively restricting the varieties to black, orange and the particularly sought-after tricoloured calico with white dominating over black and orange. The genotype in this last case will be *aaD-OoS-*, in which the *a* gene is responsible for black, *O* for orange, and *S* for spotting.

94

SPHYNX
(Hairless cat)

The case of the "hairless" cat is truly bizarre. There are occasional instances in different parts of the world of cats without fur being born into a litter of normal kittens. Considering that the best-documented cases occurred in Canada (1973) and France (1938), countries with climates certainly not warm enough for a cat devoid of fur, it would have been reasonable to study it as a scientific curiosity rather than to select it as a breed. This, however, is what has been done. The Sphynx, also known as the hairless cat, has extremely short hair, almost like fine down, and only on certain parts of the body, while the rest is bare. It has short or no whiskers. This is caused by the recessive *hr* gene (*h* in France). Cases of hairlessness are inherited monogenically but not always as recessives. Instances of other mammals are known with genes causing lack of hair inherited as dominant. It is not even known whether the cases registered in the world are owed to the same gene, or whether they are caused by mutations independent of each other.

The hairless cat has a slender body, a wedge-shaped head, golden, green or hazel almond-shaped eyes. Its tail is long and slim. The permitted colours for the fur and skin are the same as for the European Shorthair. This is a delicate animal which, lacking both underfur and outerfur has no protection against sudden changes of temperature or superficial injury.

Longhaired breeds

PERSIAN
(Longhairs)

The first reports of Persian or longhaired cats date from 1520. The appearance of these cats in Europe made great news because their appearance was such a novelty.

Today longhaired cats are officially classified as Persian in America, while in Britain they are called Longhairs.

The first Persian to arrive in Europe is said to have come from the Turkish city of Ankara, pronounced "Angora" in Greek.

For this reason cats with long fur were originally called Angora. They were relatively slender of body with a wedge-shaped head and large pointed ears. The hair, compared with that of the present-day Persian, was of medium length.

Because of its imposing and majestic appearance the Persian was preferred to the Angora, which has become almost extinct in the course of three centuries. Indeed, when the first recorded information

on the breeding of Persian cats appeared in 1871, Angoras were already no longer mentioned.

The Persian is therefore a modern breed, the fruit of careful artificial selection, while the Angora (the few specimens still found in their city of origin) has remained more or less unaltered. Ankara has been the birthplace not only of cats by this name, but also of other white longhaired mammals, such as the Angora rabbit, and a variety of goat

Self Blue

Self White

that produces the famous Angora wool. Angora cats have been reevaluated by Americans who have begun breeding them again, and who recognize them as a breed. The same is expected to happen in Britain in the near future. Many coat colours have been produced besides white, such as red, blue, black, and practically all the colours recognized for the Persian, except Colourpoint, Chinchilla and a few others.

At this point a particular phenomenon needs to be looked at: the Persian is an increasingly popular breed and is often subjected to the most varied crossing, in which care is taken over hair length and colour,

Bicoloured Persian

but not over general conformation which, in the Persian, must necessarily be of the robust type. Because of this there are more and more cats with long hair but with general conformation not meeting the required standards, such as the triangular shape of the head and the large ears. Breeding of the Persian has thus come full circle, and is returning to its origins.

The Angora, a product of natural selection, has long hair and a slender body. The long hair was exploited but breeders sought to alter the conformation by means of artificial selection, making it more robust and cobby, with a round flattened face: thus the Persian was produced. The cats that are casually being bred from this are very similar to the Angora of 1500. We say "casually" because this can be called neither natural nor artificial selection. Cats which live both indoors and outdoors, or only indoors, and which are protected by an owner, are not subject to natural selection in the traditional sense. The long full hair is not necessary as a protection against the cold, given that these cats have a warm place indoors in which to shelter, and is therefore not an indispensable instrument for survival. It cannot even be called artificial selection, however, because there is no action on man's part directed at obtaining this phenotype with long hair and slender body. Thus, the production of these cats is at present casual, helped by Persian toms with free access to gardens, which mate with cats from groups of strays. The result is that longhaired cats are frequently to be seen in these groups.

Let us now examine the Persian cat. The most striking characteristic is, of course, the long, silky hair. This trait is determined by the homozygous recessive pair of genes *ll*, together with many others that contribute to the formation of fur, which is not only long but also thick, and of the consis-

Chinchilla Persian

101

tency of silk: it is the classic case of polygenetic inheritance. A Persian must have well-furred cheeks, a full and imposing ruff covering his neck and shoulders, and a full tail, especially at the tip.

All the colours allowed for the European Shorthair are permitted for the Persian; colour therefore, does not greatly influence the characterization of the breed, the type of hair and general conformation being much more important. The coat pattern of the Longhaired Tabby, whether classic or mackerel, is less well-defined than that of the Shorthaired Tabby because of the overlapping hairs which obscure the pattern by blending the colour tones.

The general conformation of the Persian is robust: the body is cobby, the legs short and sturdy, the muscles well-developed. The overall impression must be of stockiness, which is the most important characteristic of the breed. The head must be round, broad, and with a flattened nose. The small ears with rounded tips, the large, round eyes, and the strong tail ending in a plume of fur complete the picture. This makes the overall aspect of the Persian extremely imposing.

The Persian's character matches perfectly with its physical attributes: it is noble, aloof, and quiet. It is affectionate and good-natured.

COLOURPOINT

Himalayan

The Colourpoint, known as the Himalayan in some parts of the world, should not be regarded simply as a longhaired Siamese: the physical conformation differs completely from that of the Siamese, and closely approaches that of the Persian. The body structure is robust, the legs short and muscular, the general aspect stocky. The head is broad, almost square, the face flattened, the eyes round and always blue, the ears small and set well apart, never pointed. The tail ends in a plume of hair.

Considered to be a variety of Persian, the Colourpoint was not given a breed number until 1955 in Britain, and 1957 in America.

This very beautiful cat has the typical colouring of the Siamese, the body colour being lighter than that of the points. Here too the deposition of pigment is possibly temperature dependent (see Siamese and Burmese).

The Colourpoint has an excellent character and is therefore very suitable as a pet. It is calm, affectionate and good-natured like the Persian, with moments of unpredictability that recall the Siamese. Unlike the Persian it is an excellent mouser.

Blue Point

BIRMAN

The Birman's coat colour is similar to that of the Colourpoint (probably also temperature-dependent), with the extremities darker than the body colour.

The general conformation of this breed is medium-size, the head wide, round, and full-cheeked, the eyes round, and china blue, the ears not too large. The fur is not always as long and thick as that of the Colourpoint: cats with hair of medium length are accepted. There is a shorthaired variety of Birman called Snowshoe, but it is not recognized in all countries.

The main characteristic of the breed is the presence of a pure white "glove," on each foot. This trait is hard to maintain due to the difficulty of obtaining just the correct amount of white, which is determined by the S gene (see European Bicoloured). This gene produces widely differing phenotypes, from the Self White to that with little white spots, through all the intermediate stages. The problem, then, rests with the S gene because white in the Birman must be limited to "gloves": "stockings" are not permitted by the Cat Fancy.

The Birman's origins are surrounded by fascinating legend; two in particular are of interest. The first tells how the Birman, known as the "Sacred Cat of Burma," was born before the coming of Buddha, and was venerated for centuries, jealously guarded by the Dalai Lamas and their priests. In 1918 an American millionaire succeeded in buying two Birmans from a disloyal servant and took them to America.

The second legend tells of a holy man living alone in the mountains of Indo-China with only a white cat for company. He died at the feet of a gold statue of a goddess with eyes of sapphire. The old man's soul passed into the cat, which became the colour of gold with sapphire-coloured eyes, but its paws, which were resting on the body of its beloved master, stayed as white as snow. The breed was officially recognized in France in 1925.

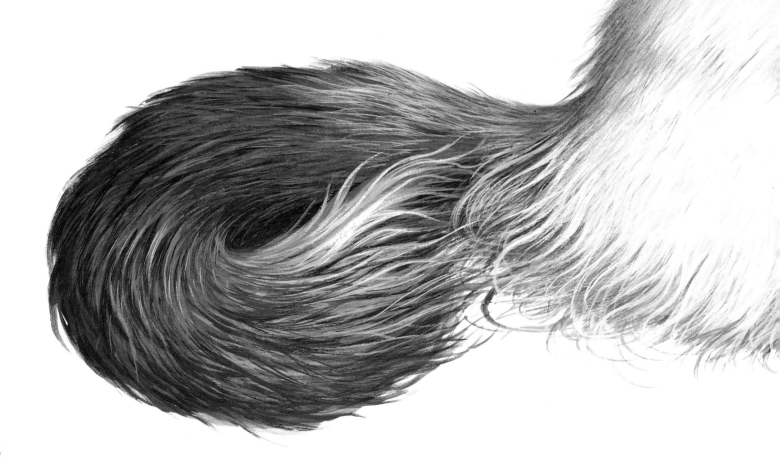

Birman

BALINESE

Contrary to what the name might suggest, the origins of this cat are not connected with Bali. It was initially called the Longhaired Siamese, but following protests by breeders of Siamese, a new name was found. The first recorded Balinese was born in a litter of Siamese in the 1950s in America; it had a longer coat than usual. Its direct relationship to the Siamese has therefore been evident from the beginning.

Unfortunately we are as yet unable to symbolize the genetic constitution of this variety. In practice, being a Longhaired Siamese, its genotype would have the identical formulae as that of the Colourpoint. The physical differences are above all in respect of body structure. The genetic basis for characteristics such as slim body, long legs, slender tail, wedge-shaped head, prominent nose, pointed ears and slanting blue eyes is so far unknown. This, in fact, is the phenotype of the Balinese, together with hair of medium length and the absence of a ruff. Temperamentally, they are less demanding than the Siamese, intelligent and extremely affectionate. A further advantage is that their coats require little attention.

Seal Point Balinese

108

Blue Point Balinese

MAINE COON

The selection operated in the breeding of the Maine Coon has not led to the results obtained with the Persian. While this is a longhaired cat it has, characteristically, short hair on the head which gradually becomes longer over the chest, shoulders and body. The tail is long and full but blunt-ended. This indicates that while being genotypically *ll* the Maine Coon lacks some of the modifying genes (bearing in mind that several different genes are responsible for hair development) which in the Persian also cause the thick, long fur on the head and neck.

This cat was called "coon" because of the biologically impossible legend that it was the result of matings between cats and raccoons, through the resemblance of its fur to that of the latter. To the progressive increase of length of hair, which is quite thick and shaggy, from the head down the body, are added the large ears with tufts of hair, the long, muscular body, the round head and the slightly oval eyes. The nose is not flattened like that of the Persian but quite long, more like that of the Angora. The coat colours are the same as those for the European Shorthair and the colour of the eyes must harmonize.

There are morphological differences between the Maine Coon and the Persian which concern not only the length of the fur, and shape of the nose, but also the expression, which is less aloof in the Maine Coon. These are differences, however, which hang by a thread, and which could disappear in a few generations of hybrids (products of crosses between Persians and Maine Coons).

Maine Coons are said to have been brought to Maine in the United States, from Turkey, in the nineteenth century.

TURKISH CAT

(Van)

This cat is believed to have originated in the Turkish region around Lake Van and to have remained for the most part unaltered, even to the extent of retaining its habit of swimming. It is a graceful cat; its long hair is completely white on the body, and it has two red patches on the forehead in front of the ears and above the eyes, like large eyebrows. The tail is also red, ringed with darker red. It is a bicoloured cat which must present the red (dark auburn) colouring distributed on the head and tail; individuals with red patches on the body are not recognized as belonging to the Turkish breed. Its coat is somewhat resistant to the process of artificial selection because it owes some of its characteristics to the S gene, the effects of which are difficult to control (see the Birman and the European Bicoloured).

In its genotype S must be present as a homozygous pair (the only such case in bicoloureds): $aaD\text{-}llOSS$ for the male and $aaD\text{-}llOOSS$ for the female. The white colour must extend over the whole body and not be limited to a few patches. The colour of the eyes is amber-yellow. Its body is similar to that of the Angora: slender but muscular, less thickset than the Persian; the head is short and wedge-shaped, the eyes almond-shaped, the ears large and upright with rounded tips, and tufts of white hair. The skin colour is pink.

SOMALI

The Somali cat is a longhaired Abyssinian. Its name, which it was given in America, is purely fanciful, and not at all indicative of its place of origin: no longhaired cats have been imported from Somalia. It is not clear whether the Somali cat originated by way of spontaneous mutations or by cross-breeding between Abyssinians and Persians. The first Somalis were recorded in America between the end of the nineteenth and the beginning of the twentieth century. The physical conformation of the Somali is slender; the body is slim, the legs long, the head round with a long nose, the ears wide and set well apart. The eyes are almond-shaped, green or amber. In character it is very similar to the Abyssinian. It is lively and intelligent, and is not suited to apartment life with no access to a garden. It is a good hunter. The colour of the kittens at birth is darker than that of the adults. Only when the cat completes its physical development does the colour take on its definitive characteristics. At present two colours are known: the normal ruddy and red. The coat does not have the fullness of other longhairs because it lacks the modifying gene for extra length.

114

CYMRIC

There are two conflicting theories regarding the origins of this cat. Some say that it was intentionally produced in America by a programme of crosses between Manxes and Persians, and that the name does not therefore indicate its origin: others maintain that in Canada, in the 1960s, a cat without a tail, and with long hair appeared casually by spontaneous mutation in a litter of Manx kittens which were of careful pedigree. In this case the name Cymric is appropriate because it proclaims the place of origin, the Isle of Man in the Irish Sea, halfway between Ireland and Wales.

Cymric is, in fact, a Celtic word meaning "Welsh." This is a tailless longhaired cat. Genetically, therefore, it will be *llMm*, plus the pair of alleles responsible for coat colour, which are the same as for the European Shorthair.

Genetically the Cymric presents the same characteristics as the Manx. Take care therefore to avoid uncontrolled matings: these may give rise to the same problems as those described for the Manx cat. The genetic anomaly is caused by the *M* gene, which is lethal when present as a homozygous pair *MM* (see p.88).

Living with a cat

The cat comes to stay

I t must be stressed how valuable and important an experience it is to be able to share one's home with animals of another species, yet without restraining, imprisoning them, taking away their liberty, or dominating them. Sharing the surroundings in which we live has been possible with few domestic animals, and among these the cat and the dog most certainly take the lead.

It is important to remember that these animals are first and foremost living creatures and not playthings for our entertainment. They have their own particular needs, and since it is we who invite them into our homes, it is our responsibility to learn what these needs are, and respect them. No one would ever entertain the idea that a wild animal such as a bear or a lion could live inside a house because their requirements are too complex, primarily in terms of space and food. A dog or cat, on the other hand, has needs which can easily be met but which, at the same time, must neither be underestimated nor exaggerated. Anyone deciding to take in a cat must first of all realize that it needs affection and attention; the rest will fall into place. For a

long time it was thought (and consequently acted upon) that the cat was a self-sufficient animal, egotistic, individualistic, and solitary. This is not in fact true. A cat that lives in the country may be relatively self-sufficient, but not in all things, for while it is true that it can hunt and eat its own prey, it still needs a place of shelter from the cold. Neither is it true, among other things, that a hungry cat catches more than a well-fed cat. Hunting requires great expenditure of energy which an undernourished cat can ill afford. He will hunt only what he needs to survive.

A cat in good health on the contrary (this does not mean overfed or fat), can be an excellent mouser or rat-catcher because it can develop to the full the gifts of predator inherent in it. In such cases, cats often do not eat their prey, but carry it off to lay at their owner's feet, almost as if it were a gift.

A cat living in an apartment must obviously be fed regularly since it has no opportunity to hunt. Leftovers from the table must not be its only source of food as they are usually too highly seasoned. Certain leftovers can be included as part of the diet, but if the cat is undernourished it will naturally try to steal whatever comes within its reach.

Apart from the correct type and quantity of food that a cat requires (remember also not to overfeed, since a cat in an apartment takes little exercise and may become overweight), it must also have a place to sleep, and fresh water available at all times. Its food plate or bowl must always be clean, since the cat is a fastidious creature. A plastic litter box or tray containing a fairly deep layer of sawdust or, better still, commercially available cat-litter should be put down for cats that do not have access to a garden. Litter trays can be bought from pet

Choosing a cat bed

When a cat first arrives in its new home it is important to have ready a special bed of its own where it can sleep undisturbed during the day and at night. It makes good sense to discipline the cat in this way, while it is young if possible. Prepare a bed that is comfortable, and easy to clean, using soft materials that will not absorb dampness from the surroundings. Choose a container just large enough for a medium-sized cat. Baskets in wicker or plastic, designed specifically for cats, and sold in pet shops or large stores are excellent, but cardboard or wooden boxes will serve the purpose equally well. Do not line it with material that is too soft, such as cottonwool. An old woollen blanket will do very well. When the box gets dirty, wash it if possible, or replace it. Cats are extremely fastidious and will not sleep on an unclean bed. Remember also that cats are very independent, and will not necessarily sleep where you would like them to, however luxurious you have made their bed. If possible, do not allow it to sleep on your own bed or in places where it could accidentally be shut in, such as a wardrobe.

shops and most hardware stores or supermarkets. The litter must be changed daily as a cat will not use a dirty litter tray.

A brush for the fur is essential for longhaired cats, which need to be brushed once a day. If this is not done their fur gets tangled, forming uncomfortable clumps; more seriously still, the cat may swallow a large amount of fur while it is licking itself clean. This can be extremely dangerous if the fur obstructs the intestines, in which case surgery may even be required. Obviously shorthaired cats need less brushing, although it is still a good thing to groom them from time to time, especially when they are moulting.

Regular checks by a vet are also necessary to make sure that the cat is vaccinated against certain illnesses, in particular cat 'flu which, once contracted, can be fatal.

The dilemma of whether to choose a male or female, street cat or thoroughbred, depends solely on what you want from your cat. Every choice has its pros and cons, which will also depend on where the cat is to live. Living in the country can present problems of pregnancy for the female (unless, of course she is spayed), but has the advantage that she will rarely stray far, and, as she grows old, will most probably be a tranquil and contented companion for her owner. A male can be a problem in other ways, often disappearing because his vagabond nature leads him constantly into danger (hunting, other animals, traffic, etc.). For those living in apartments the female can be trouble-some when on heat, but, unlike a male cat, has the great advantage of not marking her territory by spraying. All of these problems can be solved by spaying or neutering, a relatively simple operation which, as we shall discuss later, causes no harm or trauma to the animal.

When deciding on the type of cat to choose, several considerations should be borne in mind. All cats are intelligent, and although the artificial selection carried out by man may have produced breeds that are more lively or more placid than others, more intrusive or more reserved, the cat's basic intelligence has not been affected.

Longhaired thoroughbreds require careful grooming, their health is delicate, they are less productive, and often present prob-

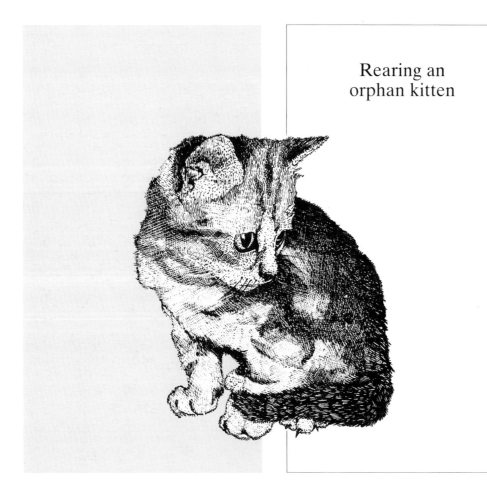

Rearing an orphan kitten

If the milk production of the mother stops or is insufficient before the kittens are weaned, that is, during the first forty-five days of their life, or if the mother dies through illness or accident, or if kittens are found abandoned at the roadside, speedy intervention is necessary. If the kittens still have their eyes closed, and the umbilical cord is attached, they will be less than ten days old. In this case the most sensible thing to do, though it may seem sad, is to have them put down painlessly by a vet since their chances of survival at this stage, even with every possible attention, are slim. It is more charitable to spare them what would otherwise be a more painful, and slower end. Besides which, those that do survive may present physical and behavioural abnormalities in adulthood.

If, on the other hand, motherless kittens are more than fifteen days old, raising them can be attempted, even though they are not yet able to ingest solid food. It is as well to remember, however, that this is a very time-consuming undertaking which may not necessarily be successful. Cow's milk is not sufficiently nutritional, not even whole

Now
as then

lems when giving birth. They are, however, extremely majestic and graceful. Ordinary street cats, on the contrary, are prolific, usually enjoy good health, and generally have fewer special needs. Nevertheless, all cats need attention and affection from their owners. Even the most uncompromising wanderer will suffer if left too much alone, and never given a friendly stroke.

A final characteristic that must be stressed; all cats enjoy play, and are great companions for their owner, from the precious Blue Persian, enobled by the highest pedigree, to the humble tabby stray picked up in the street.

Despite its small size, and its suitability to domestication, the cat is undeniably a perfect representative of the feline family, with no less of the wildness of the tiger, or the fascination of the lion. It is important to remember its origins, and try to understand its wild instincts.

Even in domestic surroundings all pets retain many of the natural instincts they display in the wild because, to a certain extent, they "bring with them" behaviour patterns they would adopt in their natural habitat.

However old the cat's association with man may be, in other words, however long ago the process of domestication may have begun, and with it the cat's entry into the household, the fact remains that to this day

all domestic animals retain unaltered certain elements of their wild behaviour patterns, even though they may no longer serve their original purpose. For the cat this is true more so perhaps than for other animals. As we have already mentioned, the cat is part of the family of Felidae, which is noted for the untameability of its members: it is already quite surprising that one of them should live peacefully alongside us.

The origins of many of the domestic cat's characteristics – irritating or fascinating, and at times incomprehensible to our eyes – must be looked for in its ancestry, that is, in the evolution of *Felis catus*. To illustrate the point, if a cat has recently had kittens, however calm and contented she may normally be, petted and spoilt by the whole family, and however deep her trust in them, she will start to move her kittens around the house in search of new "nests" some days after giving birth. Discouraging her from doing this, or trying to tempt her to use a more suitable place for the kittens' upbringing, if only for reasons of convenience and to avoid upheaval to the family's domestic routine, will not work: the cat will continue regardless, no doubt driving her owners to despair, setting her kittens down in the most inaccessible and inconceivable of places. Then, all of a sudden, when the kittens are about three or four weeks old, this

milk: the safest and simplest solution is to go to a pet shop that stocks powdered milk produced specifically for cats and dogs. This mixture will include the extra vitamins and minerals necessary to the development of the kitten. The package will also provide clear instructions on the daily quantity of milk to be given, on the basis of the weight

and age of the animal. Special feeding bottles are also available, otherwise you can use an eye dropper, although this will slow down the flow of the milk. When the kitten is small it should be fed every two or three hours; as it grows the gap between feeds can be increased. It is absolutely essential to consult a vet to check that a kitten being reared without its mother's care is developing normally. The vet will be able to recommend whether any extra items need to be added to the diet (calcium, vitamins, etc.). It is most important for the kitten to be kept warm, and be provided with a comfortable, draught-free bed, especially if it has been separated from its siblings. The kitten should normally be fully weaned between forty-five and sixty days of age. Begin by giving small quantities of baby food to make the transition from liquid to solid food as gradual as possible. After about a week, or as soon as the cat shows that it has taken to it, gradually begin to substitute the baby food with small pieces of meat, boiled fish, cereals, a little rice, green vegetables, etc. See p.124 for further information on dietary needs.

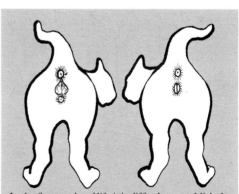

In the first weeks of life it is difficult to establish the sex of a kitten. To distinguish a male from a female look at the anal aperture. Females have less space between the anus and the vulva. Males have more space, between which the testicles will develop.

moving about will stop, and with it the mother's anxiety, not to mention that of the rest of the family, worried about tripping over kittens or finding them tucked away in the darkest corner of the wardrobe.

The cat's behaviour in such circumstances is easily understandable if one thinks of the type of surroundings in which the species evolved. Keeping the same lair for too long in the wild (in woods or forest) would be a great disadvantage for a cat with three or four defenseless kittens, and with the need to go out and hunt in order to survive. The entrance to the lair, and the lair itself would be impregnated with the smell of the occupants, not to mention the mewing of the newly-born, which would certainly be audible, and attract attention from a considerable distance. All this would present an invitation to predators which, if the mother and her kittens stayed for too long in the same place, could easily track them down. Both in the domestic cat and in the wildcat the female rears her kittens without the help of the male; every departure from the lair, to hunt for food, for example, is therefore dangerous for the kittens' survival, since they are instantly threatened by predators. This frequent moving of the kittens, especially in the first weeks of their life when they are totally helpless, is a defense strategy on the part of the mother.

In other words, such behaviour made the cat better "adapted" to that particular environment by decreasing the chances of the offspring's being found and killed, the result being that it was able to reproduce more successfully than animals that did not adopt the same behaviour.

This is how natural selection works: animals are not aware of the advantages of their actions, but if one form of behaviour is more advantageous than another *in particular surroundings*, the animal adopting it will survive and reproduce better; this pattern of behaviour is then transmitted to the next generation which, in turn, will pass it on to the next, and so on.

As changes in the environment occur animals gradually adapt to them. If the environment changes slowly, biological

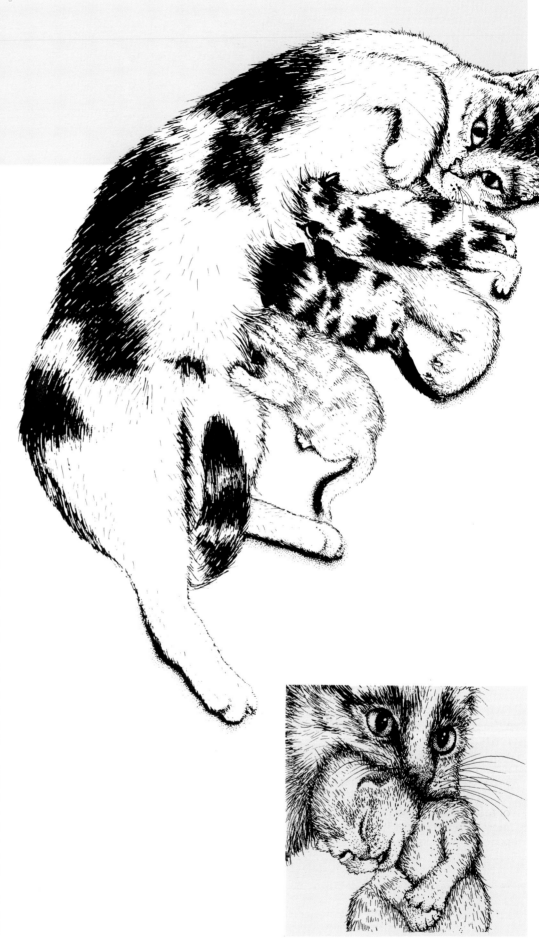

evolution may keep pace, other, more suitable genes generally becoming favoured by natural selection. Such is not the case, however, with the cat. Like other domestic animals it found itself, almost at a stroke, living in a completely different environment from its original one. It has therefore retained many habits which, in its original surroundings, would have been "adaptive," but which have now lost their function. Domesticated cats feel safe at home, they encounter no predators, do not have to hunt for their food, and yet for a certain time they will continue to move their young *because they have been selected to do so*. This behaviour pattern (and by the same token, others) will sooner or later disappear because they will no longer be advantageous to the animal; but this will take time. There are many other habits, besides this particular one, involving nearly all the cats' activities; it is interesting to examine a few of them more closely.

We live with cats; we know many of their habits, but perhaps we are not always able to understand their function.

There is, for example, a difference between intra-specific and inter-specific communication, in other words, communications between animals of the same species, and between animals of different species. Some behaviour patterns displayed by cats are directed at other cats, and contain signals that only they are able to sense. A typical example of this is territory-marking, which will be dealt with in detail later. When a cat marks its territory it is sending a message to other members of its species; this kind of signal would certainly not be intended for humans.

In certain other situations, however, its express purpose is to communicate with its owner; for example, when a cat purrs because it is being caressed, or when it rubs itself against your legs. In the first case it is expressing contentment, in the second the rubbing may signify a request, either for food or simply for attention.

Looking at the different ways in which a cat expresses itself, it is interesting to note that most of the methods used in inter-specific communication (between cat and man) are part of the behaviour repertoire of intra-specific communication (cat to cat). So, in most cases, the cat "borrows" modes of expression used with its fellow felines, and uses them to communicate with man. Often these are infantile habits which persist into adulthood. In explanation of this phenomenon it is argued that the cat regards its owner as its mother, and in communicating with its owner, however adult the cat may be, it adopts the infantile behaviour typical of the species.

This theory is open to criticism because it is equally true that, in certain cases, adult cats use infantile behaviour to communicate among themselves, for example when they are demonstrating friendship toward members of the same social group. Typical is the raised tail during the nose-to-nose contact of reciprocal recognition. Infantile behaviour (just as physical infantile

Weaning

When a cat gives birth and suckles her kittens normally, there are not many problems for the family to which she belongs. After the first forty-five days the mother becomes less and less available to their continued demands. From as early as four weeks the process of *weaning* can begin. If the cat has free access to the garden she may occasionally return with small prey such as a bird or mouse, and put it down in front of her kittens. This is her way of teaching them to accept solid foods. The mother will gradually begin to take pieces of food from her bowl, and carry them to her kittens, tempting them to eat. Kittens learn most things by imitation, and generally begin to eat solid food without the owner even noticing. One way you can help is to provide softer food than usual, since kittens' teeth are still not very strong. With regard to the use of the litter tray, on the other hand, the mother's guidance is not always sufficient: she will use it herself in front of the kittens, but will not physically carry them to it. It is important for the owner gently but firmly to scold a kitten if it soils any part of the house. Immediately afterwards the kitten must be picked up and taken to the litter tray; it will very soon learn to use it for the appropriate purpose.

Food

To keep your cat healthy and fit a well-balanced diet is essential.

1 – An adult cat needs, on average, 6-8 oz (175-225 g) of food per day.

2 – Since the cat is a carnivore, the diet should include meat and fish, but this does not mean that it should consist *only* of meat and fish. It should be well-balanced and varied, and should not encourage the cat to have preferences. Fish should always be cooked, firstly because it is more digestible in this form, and secondly because some fish contains substances which are harmful to cats, and which are eliminated through cooking. Beef can be given cooked or raw; both ways have their advantages and disadvantages. Raw meat is more digestible and, given in small pieces (not minced), provides very good exercise for the jaws, helping to remove food remains and tartar from the gums. However, it has the possible disadvantage of causing food poisoning or worms if it contains bacteria. This danger is even greater with pork, which must *never* be given raw.

3 – Occasionally it is a good thing to give the cat a bone with a little meat attached. If you give your cat a chicken bone be extremely careful, as they splinter easily, and can get lodged in the cat's throat or stomach. It must therefore be large enough not to be able to be swallowed or splintered with the teeth. Thin bones and bone fragments can cause the animal to choke and even die. The same is true of fish and rabbit bones.

4 – Never give a cat spicy food, sweets or sausages.

5 – Not all cats like milk; it is essential for kittens, but not for adults. Never force an adult cat to take milk if it refuses, since cats are rarely capricious without reason: many cats are physically unable to tolerate milk, and in others it can cause diarrhoea.

6 – Cats living in apartments should be given certain kinds of grass which, in the wild, they ingest regularly as an emetic. Pots of a mixture of grasses can be prepared by sowing seeds of common grass, barley or rye grass. Some cats love parsley.

7 – A teaspoon of vegetable oil (sunflower, peanut or olive oil) every so often, either spooned directly into the mouth or otherwise sprinkled on to the food, helps the elimination from the intestine of fur balls caused by the cat's daily fur-licking. This is particularly important for longhaired cats.

8 – One gram per day of yeast provides an excellent source of vitamins (B_1 and B_2).

9 – Aways provide a bowl of fresh water. Although cats drink little, water is an essential part of their diet, much more so than milk.

Recommended foods for cats

— meat;

— fish;

— small pieces (2.5 in/1 cm) of raw liver, heart, etc., but not too often since they are very rich;

— canned food; (some cats are unable to digest it);

— cheese; avoid fancy cheeses and those with plastic rinds;

— pasta mixed with meat or fish;

— yolk of hardboiled egg, but not more than one a week;

— cooked vegetables in small quantities, mixed with meat or fish: asparagus, cauliflower, spinach, lettuce, green beans, carrots;

— dry cat food (biscuits and shapes); given in very small quantities, these are useful for cleaning the teeth and provide good exercise for the jaws.

characteristics) that is linked to the suppression of aggressiveness during encounters with other individuals of the same species is most probably an integral part of friendly behaviour, whether intra-specific or inter-specific.

An extremely interesting phenomenon is the development of efforts by the cat at direct communication aimed solely at the owner, a phenomenon which is never seen between cats themselves. These attempts do not yet constitute true rituals with a definite stereotyped sequence, but represent behaviour that shows the cats' aim to communicate with a human being, and not with another cat. Anyone with a cat that has given birth at home will have been through this experience. For example, one can quite

Training

Although notoriously independent animals, cats can be educated or trained, and it is important to teach them right from wrong as early as possible.

Training (in the sense of disciplining) a cat is not such a difficult task: cats are very intelligent, and quick to understand what humans may approve or disapprove of in their behaviour; in fact, they often adopt the attitude of one who expects a scolding, thereby advertising their misdeeds, even before they are discovered. Educating a cat does not involve rewards and punishments; it is achieved instead by establishing a clear and firm relationship from the outset. There is never any need for excess: it is pointless, for example, to tempt a cat with tidbits because it will not understand that these are rewards for good behaviour, and will immediately assume that they are to be part of its normal diet. Cats are unable to grasp the concept of "prize" because they rarely do anything against their will, even for gain.

Striking an animal is not advisable either, as the only likely effect is that it will arouse suddenly find oneself with a pregnant cat, its big eyes opened wide in expectation. A glance at her still full plate excludes the idea of a request for food; a quick look at the calendar, and a rapid calculation of the number of weeks since her mating will tell you that the cat is about to give birth. By a phenomenon as yet unexplained in evolutionary terms (cats in the wild give birth unaided, and even hide themselves away for the event), a domestic cat on the other hand may want the help of her owner during the birth of her kittens, or at least want her owner to be present at the time. The cat therefore has to find a way of making you understand what only she knows, and that is when she is about to deliver. Since the behavioural repertoire of

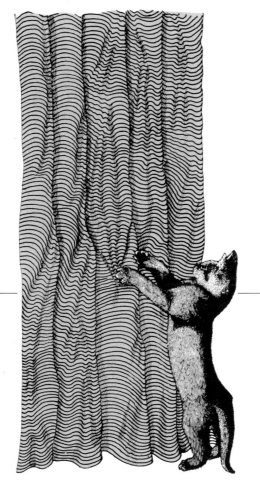

the species does not include this eventuality, cats make every conceivable effort to explain it. Some will follow their owner everywhere, eyes wide open, others will mew weakly, taking a few steps toward their basket, turning round to check that their owner is following them; others will lie down and stretch out, usually in a place impregnated with familiar human smells, for example on its owner's bed, and quietly await the moment of birth. They will go to great lengths to make us understand that we must be present at the event: cats have even been known to attempt to get up and follow their owner, even after they have started to give birth if they see that they have any intention of going away.

in the cat a feeling of revulsion toward its owner who has used his superior strength to inflict pain. Repairing such psychological damage can take months or even years. The kind of "dialogue" that should be set up with your cat can be based on a few precise but simple rules.

First of all, call your cat by name, and use it every time you want to attract its attention. Choose a short, fairly simple name; the cat will quickly get used to it, and respond to your call. Another important rule is to make clear your disapproval when a cat does something wrong: a short "No," or a

few words, spoken firmly but without shouting, every time the cat repeats the action will soon make it understand that you do not approve of its behaviour. But you must scold it every time, or it will not get the message. Unfortunately there is little point (although it is worth trying) scolding a tomcat if it urinates around the house to mark its territory; to the cat this is the right thing to do to safeguard its "home." On the other hand, if you catch it urinating or excreting in a crouching position outside the litter box (an action which has nothing to do with its territory), you

should scold it firmly. Also, do not make the mistake of rubbing its nose in its faeces: the cat might confuse the association of that particular smell with that place, and continue to use it for that purpose. Make sure that no trace of the odour remains by carefully washing the surface with disinfectant mixed with water.

If you want to teach your cat to use a scratching post scold it the instant you find it clawing the furniture, the carpets or the curtains; then pick it up, carry it to the post, and place its paws on it. Be patient: sooner or later it will understand. Never compromise over anything taken from the kitchen or the table. Scold the cat straight away and do not allow it to eat the stolen food.

One last piece of advice: teach the cat two or three other words besides its name. Simple words like "food," "eat," and "down" are within its range of comprehension. If used at the right moment they will become associated with the appropriate behaviour, and it will be a source of pride to see the cat's prompt reaction.

Communication
with humans

I n ordinary parlance "to purr" is used jokingly as synonymous with "to show a feeling of pleasure," when one is contented, relaxed or happy. And this is in fact its function. Even kittens that are only a few days old are already able to purr. As soon as they are able to find their mother's teat – groping their way to it since their eyes are still closed – they show their contentment by purring, which is a surprisingly loud noise considering the size of the kittens producing it. The mechanism by which cats produce this sound is not yet understood. Certainly they use the air they breathe both in and out, probably to vibrate the vocal cords, but the theory that they use other organs (the vena cava, for example) is not excluded.

Purring is a sound signal developed primarily to tell the mother of the offspring's

state of contentment and good health. Kittens purr not only when suckling but also when their mother licks them clean. Another behaviour pattern in kittens when suckling is the rhythmical pressing of alternate paws against the mother's stomach in the area around the teats. This behaviour stimulates the mother and helps the flow of milk; it is an instinctive and mechanical action which at the same time communicates a state of well-being. This particular behaviour is also found in the adult, although it no longer serves the same purpose: it is still related to purring as in the newly-born, but becomes another way of manifesting happiness and well-being. Compare the rhythmical pawing movements of suckling kittens to those of your cat as it purrs in response to your caress: the movement is the same, and the message the animal is conveying is one of contentment at being stroked. This is an example of

infantile behaviour persisting in the adult as a means of communication.

Another interesting example of this phenomenon is seen when the animal is requesting food. As soon as a kitten is able to walk, usually from about thirty days onward, it develops a very particular way of asking its mother for milk; it will pass round and round the queen, rubbing its body against hers. Its body is slightly arched, the tail held straight. It will stretch out its head, and try to rub it under the mother's chin with a movement beginning with the nose and ending with the area between the ears. Sometimes the sequence is accompanied by purring. This behaviour is mainly adopted when the kitten is seeking food, but also attention. Whatever the motive, it is always a gesture. Indeed, the mother will at times respond by stretching out to let the kitten suck her milk, and at others she will lick it affectionately.

In the adult cat the same behaviour can be observed, directed especially toward the owner, but also toward other members of the family. Typical of the request for food is the tail held absolutely upright with a slightly relaxed tip. Try it out: call your cat from another room, making it understand that it is time to eat, perhaps by showing it its bowl from a distance; it will arrive at a run, with its tail held upright, and will keep it in that position until food is put in front of it. The same posture can be seen in stray cats swarming around whoever is giving them food.

The tail is often held straight while the cat, awaiting a meal, rubs itself against the legs of the person getting it ready. It is going through the same motions as a kitten asking for its mother's attention, pressing its head against its owner's legs so that its back

Features of the adult and its young

arches, rubbing itself and finally wrapping its tail around them. An identical sequence is used when the cat wants attention, and it is often accompanied by attempts to slip its nose under its owner's hand and by pawing movements with the feet.

Along with other behaviour patterns the straight tail belongs to the group of attitudes indicating friendly intentions. Two members of the same social group acknowledging one another in a nose-to-nose contact will at the same time keep their tails straight up. If the tail is totally straight, without the relaxed tip, it usually shows indifference. The opposite behaviour is found in non-amicable situations: when adopting a threatening posture, the cat keeps its tail low and slightly bent, flicking it

from side to side; in a defensive posture the tail is held as close as possible to the body.

That the position of the tail indicates the attitude of the cat to those around it is proved also by the fact that a young cat (male or female) holds it rigidly straight when it meets a strange adult. A young cat always feels vulnerable before an adult cat, and therefore adopts a submissive rather than aggressive posture.

To sum up, a great deal of infantile behaviour is found in adult cats, both when they are communicating with one another and when communicating with humans. In both instances it serves to indicate a friendly state of mind and to inhibit aggressiveness. It has been shown that the infantile traits of almost all animal species serve

the same purpose: however, animals cannot generally make use of them indefinitely as their behaviour naturally changes with age. This is not so with infantile behaviour that can easily be retained into adulthood. The adults imitate the ways of their young, and in certain cases this behaviour forms part of stereotyped sequences that become known as "rituals." In some species of bird for example, during courting, and when asking for food, the female assumes the attitude used by young birds that have not yet left the nest. She does not actually want to be fed: the purpose of the infantile conduct is to demonstrate her own availability for mating. This conduct now forms part of the behavioural repertoire of the species: all females exhibit it.

Treacherous cat?

Q uite often when you are stroking your cat, who may even be purring blissfully at the time, he will unexpectedly and suddenly turn, and bite the hand that strokes it. This has given rise to its reputation for treachery. This sudden change in behaviour is unlikely to happen when the cat is lying stretched out, relaxed, blissfully drowsy. It happens more commonly when the cat is sitting or standing and being stroked, or, even more likely, when it is winding itself about the person stroking it. The explanation is linked to the fact that the cat is a Felid, a member therefore, of a family of wild animals for which friendly physical contact with another of the same species, not for the purpose of reproduction, is a fairly rare event; even in a social species such as lions, which sleep close to one another, it is unusual for them to actually make contact, and for this to occur with a member of another species is absolutely unthinkable. Some cats, not all, feel in a state of conflict if they are stroked for too long, or in a rough or forceful way: the contact is a source of pleasure, but if it is prolonged or too rough, the cat will begin to feel uneasy. The amount of adrenalin in the cats' blood increases, and it is unable to keep still. The purring becomes louder, rising to an unnatural crescendo, and every so often the cat's ears become flattened in a typical menacing attitude, and it mews. When the animal is over-excited it will bite. Quite often this is only a sign of its intention to bite gently, without closing its teeth.

This reaction naturally startles whoever is playing with the cat, and they usually stop. The interruption is enough for the cat to regain its composure. If, however, the game is continued with the same force as before, the pattern is repeated.

If you scold the cat instead, or make a movement as if to strike it with your hand, it will certainly run away. By seizing your hand in its mouth the cat finds a way out of the situation of conflict; in other words it will bite only when there is no other way of defusing the tension caused by the too close and prolonged physical contact.

Taking in an adult cat

T he behaviour of humans often directly affects the behaviour of domestic animals living with them. It goes without saying that a cat – or in fact any pet – has to suffer the consequences of its owner's every decision with regard to household management. It is important to bear this fact in mind when planning changes of any kind, and remember that the cat, too, has its own personality and particular needs.

For example, it may well happen that, for whatever reason, you are no longer in a position to keep the cat you have reared since a kitten: in this case it is your responsibility to entrust it to a reliable friend who will promise to look after it. If the opposite happens, you may well find yourself the faithful friend who is called on in the emergency, and if you accept, bear in mind that the animal you are bringing into your home will, in most cases, already be an adult with a fully developed personality and acquired habits. To help the animal settle down with

the minimum of bother, there is one simple rule of thumb: from the minute it arrives, be particularly attentive, try to understand its needs, and avoid any stressful situations, for example exposing it to too much noise if it has been used to a quiet household. In this chapter we shall discuss how an adult cat can suffer emotionally by being removed from its owner, and how, at the same time, it can feel disorientated and insecure at being taken away from its "territory." Yours may be the onerous task of helping it to get over both these traumas.

During the first few days let the new-comer become acclimatized by allowing him to explore his new home (shut off the best rooms if you are a little unsure of his habits). All cats, whether male or female, will sniff at everything because this is their way of getting to know things. Do not stop them from doing this; do, however, keep doors and windows firmly closed in case

they try to run away. If possible, ask the previous owner to give you the cat's bed or basket, its bowl or scratching post, but most importantly, its litter tray: this will be steeped in the cat's own scent, as well as that of its old home, and will reduce the animal's stress at finding itself in a place full of strange smells.

If, on the first day, the cat urinates outside the litter tray, do not scold it harshly because this could have serious effects by frightening and antagonizing the animal. Instead, take the object (if possible) on which it has urinated and put it in or near the litter tray (especially if the litter tray is new). Then bring the cat gently near to it, and leave it alone to sniff around. It will soon understand what it has done wrong.

As previously mentioned, a cat in new surroundings will be tense and nervous: loud noises frighten it because it does not know what causes them nor at what they are directed; you might call from one room to another to try to make it feel at home, but the cat may misunderstand and think you are scolding it. Pick it up if it seems to want attention, but do not force it into physical contact at first, if it seems shy. In other words be patient, and try to understand that it takes time to get used to a new place and a new person. Within a week or two he will already have found his feet, made clear his habits, and established a relationship with his new owner. Cats are very adaptable animals and will fit in to most households with very few problems.

A similar approach is necessary if you are introducing a second cat into the household. Take care not to give the new cat preferential treatment: do not let the "intruder" (this is how your present "boss cat" will see him) indiscriminately use your own cat's possessions, as this could provoke a distressing overlapping of territorial smells for both animals. Leave the two cats alone to sniff at each other as long as they want to. By doing this they establish contact which will either remain at the sniffing stage of tolerant indifference, or, more often, be the first step toward a more enduring relationship.

Territorial behaviour

A cat will inevitably regard the place it grows up in as its own property.

Just as the wild cat is a territorial animal, as we have already discussed, so is the domestic cat.

Wherever it may roam, a cat will always return to a specific place which it defends against intruders, and where it finds food and shelter.

Let us begin with the house, where the cat spends most of its time when not out at play. It is a common belief that the cat is a creature that becomes attached to places rather than people. In support of this theory there are many stories of cats that have moved with a family from the place where they were reared, and have managed, against almost incredible odds, to find their way back to the house where they lived before. This behaviour must not be interpreted too simplistically, in a way that does not take into account the behavioural characteristics of the species. The attachment of a feline to a certain place is not, in fact, emotional, but rather biological and functional.

When a cat is introduced into a house, whether it is bought from a pet shop or whether it is given to you as a gift from a friend, it is most likely to be still a kitten. We have already discussed the question of taking in an adult cat; now let us turn our attention to the kitten arriving in new surroundings.

Cats settle down very readily; they do not need a great deal of space, particularly when they are small. Their main activity at this stage is play, and so any object they come across becomes a new toy, every corner of the house a fascinating unknown world to explore.

Play and exploration (the importance of which will be discussed separately) allow the kitten to familiarize itself with its new surroundings and, whether its life is spent within the four walls of an apartment or between the house and garden, to establish the boundaries of its "territory." A cat has no choice with regard to its territory because, to a certain extent, this is imposed on it by the owner. However, this does not alter the fact that in its relationship with other cats it will develop the natural behaviour typical of the species with regard to the exclusive right and priority of access to resources within its own territory and, if it has been the only representative of the species raised in the house, intolerance of other cats. A cat raised with others is tolerant toward those it has grown up with, but together they will attack cats not belonging to their group.

This behaviour does not happen at once: a kitten initially shows curiosity about members of the species which are neither its mother nor its siblings (and this shows that from an early age they have a discriminatory capacity, and can distinguish between family and strangers). But if a cat has been brought up without others it will be difficult to impose a companion upon it in adulthood within the same house, although with the use of the right stratagems, it is not entirely impossible. This does not mean that the cat is a solitary animal: if it is allowed out it may become part of a group of cats living in the same neighbourhood. The walls of the house remain, however, the impassable frontiers of its territory because we have indirectly led it to consider them as such.

It is clear from the above that the cat does not "love" the house, does not form an affectionate attachment to places, but it feels at ease only when it is within its own territory, or when it knows that it can return to it. In addition to being a safe and familiar place, the cat's territory usually provides the food and shelter necessary for its survival. For this reason, too, it would never abandon its "patch." A cat transported suddenly to another home will be ill-at-ease, may show signs of fear or stress and want to go back. It does not understand why you have not come too, and it will only

be after it has spent a few days in solitude, that it realizes that you are not there. The bond of affection between cat and owner does exist, but it is a more recent aspect of the cat's behaviour. Nature intended the cat to seek out its own territory, and to live in it, not to find an owner. Throughout its evolution the cat's territory, and not its relationship with man, has generally been the indicator for its state of well-being. This explains a particular behaviour pattern – one which is perhaps the biggest problem for anyone with a tomcat in the house – and that is the habit of spraying small quantities of urine about the house.

Both males and females exhibit territorial behaviour, but as is the case with the wild cat it is the male in particular that has the continuous need to "mark" its territory.

This is the cat's way of putting its signature on the protected area with its own smell. Humans use the spoken and written word to communicate the fact that an object or a place belongs to them: many animals, cats among them, use other means of communication, for example, olfactory signals. The urine a cat sprays around its habitat contains chemicals (pheromones) that produce particular odours. These, in their

turn, serve to transmit certain messages to other cats. Any cat finding the scented marking, whether a tom or a queen, will stop to sniff at it carefully. This enables them to gather certain information about the individual that left it, including its sex and age, the approximate time the trace was left (minutes, hours or days earlier), and possibly even whether it is a cat they already know, or a complete stranger.

It has been observed that, in certain cases, cats use chemical signals to decide whether it is the right time to approach a particular place, or whether they should wait for a more opportune moment: if, for example, a cat comes across a trace of urine sprayed a few moments earlier, just as it is about to go into a neighbour's garden, it means that the cat that released it has just entered that area. The possible reactions may be various: the cat may wait a short time to give the other time to go away, or it may advance cautiously, conscious of the imminence of an encounter, or it may even turn back.

It has been suggested that the dominant animal, the leader, in a group spreads a different odour through its urine from that of its "subordinates." While this theory is

quite fascinating, there is little evidence to support it.

The wealth of information contained in these few drops of urine is beyond human perception because we do not possess, or rather no longer have, receptors capable of analyzing it. We are only aware of the disagreeable sensation of a nauseating and penetrating smell. The pheromones are extremely volatile substances which, as soon as they are released into the atmosphere, spread, and impregnate with their odour whatever they touch. Furthermore, in order for the marking to achieve its aim of informing other cats that this territory is exclusive to one particular animal, it must be constantly renewed. The cat will tend therefore to patrol the house regularly, spraying its urine in various places throughout the night and day. If you have a male cat it is as well to ask your friends not to bring their own cat to visit, especially if it is also a tom, as this will encourage the "boss" of the house to make it understand that this is his house by increasing the rate of territorial marking (in the wild the frequency of marking with urine is roughly one spraying every five minutes). Female cats also spray with urine every so often but it is a very rare event, and they generally do it during the period of oestrus.

If your cat's spraying presents a problem, there are two solutions: the first will reduce the number of sprayings inside the house, but not their total elimination; the second measure is more radical. The first method is to let your cat out to carry on his forays in the open. He will certainly establish relationships with the other cats in the neighbourhood, and since he will always meet them outside (never make the mistake of letting him bring strange cats inside your house), he will tend to mark the boundaries of his territory outside the walls of the house. He may sometimes relapse, and fall back into the temptation of making a few reassuring sprayings inside your home, but this should not happen often.

The second method is neutering. In general a cat will no longer spray if it has been neutered at the right age. If, however,

the operation is performed too late, when the cat has already had sexual experience or confrontations with other toms, it is possible that the habit will not altogether disappear. Consult your vet about this problem if in doubt or in need of advice.

Many people are against the idea of having their cats neutered, because they think that it might change their character, hinder their development or cause psychological damage. None of this will happen if the operation is carried out by a qualified vet, and, most importantly, at the right time (thirty-six weeks for males). By this stage the right amount of testosterone (the male hormone produced by the testicles) will have entered the blood stream to guarantee the development of certain functions, but insufficient to allow the development of certain others. The urine of tomcats begins to smell very pungent when they are four to five months old. About one or two weeks after the operation their urine starts to lose its strong smell.

A neutered cat does not undergo a personality change, does not suffer psychologically because it feels "different," and does not feel rejected by the rest of feline society. The effects of castration on adult male strays can be very different, however, as experts in animal behaviour have observed, for example, during campaigns for feline population control carried out in many large cities. During such campaigns, the adult cat is captured, neutered, then released back into its original group. The problems arising from this action can be many, and are related both to the reintroduction of the cat into the group (other cats, not recognizing the new "smell," might even kill the neutered male they now see as an intruder), and to the physiological changes brought about in a fully developed animal in which the production of a certain hormone suddenly ceases.

The advice to neuter a cat is directed at those who are able to plan the timing of the operation (in other words, you must know the age of the cat) and to those who are able to look after the cat at home after the operation.

There is a third possibility: if you are unable to let your cat outdoors, and are against the idea of having it neutered, a simpler solution is to choose a female. Raising a female cat presents far fewer problems than you think.

Cats do not only mark by spraying urine. The following behaviour patterns are exhibited by both males and females. As well as spraying to mark their territory, cats sometimes use secretions produced by sebaceous glands located in various parts of the body. These glands are found under the chin, along the line of the jaw. The secretion produced is colourless, viscous and, to humans, odourless. Obviously it is not so for cats.

The habit of marking by means of the secretions produced by the sub-mandibulary glands is more rare than the use of urine. The cat usually places the side of its face against an object (indoors this may be a table-leg, the corner of a piece of furniture, etc, outdoors it may be a wall or fence) and, with a movement from the point of the nose to the back of the cheek, rubs itself several times against the object, releasing its own particular scent. Some experts maintain that there are also glands for the production of secretions for marking both territory and social companions (other members of the group) between the pads of the paws, on the temples, and at the base of the tail. In support of this, cats can be seen pressing their head against the legs of their owner or against the body of another cat, or wrapping their tail around them. Scratching tree trunks or, if there is no tree available, clawing the furniture or carpet, is another way in which cats mark territory with their own particular scent; however, at present these are only hypotheses that require further research and study.

It is also thought that scratching objects serves the dual purpose of providing visual communication, as if the cat wished to leave his mark as well as his scent on the objects in his territory.

Given the irregularity in terms of distance and in the infrequency with which it occurs, this behaviour need not necessarily be linked with territorial marking, but might simply be related instead to the occasional need to sharpen or wear down the claws. Some cats use their claws much less than others. Cats kept in apartments, for example, need to scratch objects more regularly than those that are able to go outdoors, because housebound cats never have the opportunity to wear down their claws naturally.

There are also other behaviour patterns the function of which is the subject of debate. One of these is rolling on the ground. We are not of course referring to the female on heat who rolls on her back after mating, but of the times when either males or females are overwhelmingly attracted to an object giving off a particular smell, and feel the irresistible urge to roll on it. There are many examples of such behaviour: from the body of a long-dead bird or other small animal found in the garden, to the shoes of the owner, recently returned from a walk in the country. There is as yet no scientific explanation for the impulse that drives cats to roll on these objects.

More is understood about the tendency of cats to roll on the ground in other contexts. It is not a generalized behaviour pattern, but some cats roll about in front of their sexual partner or in front of an adversary after a fight. These are generally toms. In the first case, a male cat in courtship may perform before the female on heat an extremely fascinating sequence of movements consisting of a mixture of rollings on the ground, and little promenades around her. In this context his aim of attracting the attention of the object of his desire is obvious. When, on the other hand, two male cats fight, the victor sometimes engages in an extravagant display involving rolling around in front of the loser; the purpose of this is to demonstrate his invulnerability. Or does it serve to mark the cat's territory? Or is it simply the cat's way of demonstrating its physical superiority? There is no single explanation for it. One certain fact, however, is that when a cat behaves in this way, exposing its stomach to its owner, it is showing absolute trust.

The cat and other pets

Peaceful coexistence between your cat, and budgerigars or aquarium fish is possible if you follow certain basic guidelines. The main problem stems from the fact that in the wild birds and fish are the cat's normal prey. It is therefore essential to put the cage containing birds or rodents (hamsters, white mice, etc.) well out of the cat's reach; quite apart from the distress the caged animals will experience at the proximity of the cat, which can have a harmful effect in itself, the cat will usually manage to insert a paw between the bars, kill the luckless inmate, and drag it out in pieces. It is pointless to scold the cat, either before or after the event, because there are no ways of suppressing behaviour that would be the norm in its natural habitat, and which has always enabled it to survive in the wild. The cat will understand well enough that it is forbidden to kill the other animals in the house, but it is nevertheless likely to wait for a favourable opportunity to do so anyway.

Fish in an aquarium are in less danger, especially if the tank is large and cannot easily be moved. As a rule, a cat will limit itself to gazing at the fish but may, exceptionally, dip a paw into the water, although it would not always succeed in catching a fish. It must be discouraged from this kind of behaviour, however, because it could cause serious damage to the electrical equipment in the tank. Also, do not place lightweight containers or glass goldfish bowls near the edge of a table or on the flat surface of a piece of furniture. Very daring cats could push them with their weight and, having succeeded in toppling them to the ground, might eat the fish.

The simplest way to get dogs and cats to live peacefully together is to let them grow up together from the beginning. If one of the two comes into the house when the other is already an adult problems could arise. It is best to avoid bringing a kitten or, even worse, an adult cat into your home if you have a guard dog or retriever, or a dog which has shown a tendency to chase and even kill cats and other small animals. If a puppy is introduced into a household where there is already a dog, its life would not be in danger although it should not be forgotten than an adult cat can seriously hurt a small dog. In all cases, give your pets as much time as is necessary to adapt to each other. Do not force contact. Sometimes relationships of dignified indifference or tolerance will form between them, sometimes one of amicable coexistence. In sharing out your attention between the animals remember that both dogs and cats are jealous creatures.

The cat's relationship with its owner

A cat shows affection toward all members of the family, usually of different levels of intensity, but it tends to single out one particular person toward whom it will always have a special attitude. It is redundant to compare the cat's behaviour with that of the dog, and to expect similarities. The two animals are physiologically far removed, and have a completely different genetic and evolutionary history. The dog will demonstrate affection in a noisier more evident manner than the cat which, in turn, can show an exclusive attachment to one particular person and an obstinate unwillingness to transfer it elsewhere.

The affective links formed by a cat with a human being are demonstrated, for example, by the way in which it chooses his or her companion, following them around from room to room; also, by the fact that it suffers when subjected to long periods of separation, sometimes refusing to eat and appearing dejected; the affective link is demonstrated further by the fact that the cat will often wait behind the door at the hour when the owner usually returns. Moreover, if it can choose the person from whom to receive caresses it will prefer its owner, and if he or she pays attention to another animal it will show quite clearly that it is offended or jealous; finally, as already discussed earlier, a female cat about to give birth may make it clear that she needs assistance, and only in the absence of the owner will she turn to someone else.

But what is the nature of the attachment to a human being? There are many hypotheses. The most important are the theory of identification of the mother in the owner; the theory of "imprinting"; the functional theory; and the theory of the social companion. We exclude the pack leader theory, formulated principally for dogs, according to which the domestic animal sees in the owner the chief of its clan, and in consequence establishes with him or her a relationship of obedient subordination. This cannot be true of the cat, because it was not originally a social animal; the species did not organize individuals into structured groups in which there was a leader, or a dominant animal to play the rôle of the chief. On the contrary, we have seen that the wild cat, from which it is believed that the form of cat domesticated by man derives, presented the typical characteristics of a solitary animal. The domestic cat, not being naturally selected to recognize a pack leader in its natural environment, would be even less able today to attribute such a rôle to its owner.

Identification of the mother in the owner: some students of feline behaviour, including Desmond Morris, maintain that cats see the human beings that surround it as so many mother-cats. This implies that cats behave toward human beings as if they remained kittens indefinitely. However complete their physical development, and their behavioural development in their encounters with their own species, they will never realize all the character potential which would cause them to behave as adults toward humans. By this theory, therefore, the nature of the attachment to an owner is the same as that of a kitten to its mother.

This hypothesis is, however, open to question, because it has been demonstrated that in the individual relationships between members of the same social group infantile behaviour is also widely used, even when the protagonists are all adults.

This suggests that the owner-mother theory by itself is insufficient to clarify the nature of the relationship between cat and owner, otherwise it would be necessary to argue that a cat identifies its mother in any person toward whom it shows infantile behaviour, which is obviously untrue. For further information on infantile behaviour, see the section on Communication with humans, p.126.

The theory of imprinting: in psychology, "imprinting" takes the meaning of "early learning in the impressionable phase." This process of learning is genetically programmed in such a way that animals are predisposed to acquire certain notions in a particular period of their lives and in that period only. This so-called "imprinting"

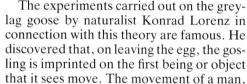

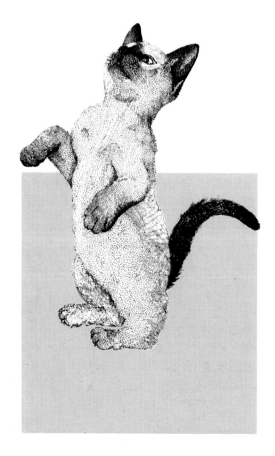

period is generally limited to one stage of their development, often just after birth.

The experiments carried out on the greylag goose by naturalist Konrad Lorenz in connection with this theory are famous. He discovered that, on leaving the egg, the gosling is imprinted on the first being or object that it sees move. The movement of a man, a goose or simply a cardboard box dragged along the ground will trigger off in the gosling the reaction of pursuit.

Once a young animal is "imprinted" on a person, animal or thing, it will show that it prefers it to its true mother. This means that the young's learning of the physical aspect of the mother (normally the first animal seen by the newly-born) is achieved in the very first moments after hatching from the egg. For the greylag goose this is the genetically programmed "sensitive," or "imprinting" period for learning who is the mother.

This type of learning, unlike others, is generally irreversible, does not require rewards, but is reinforced by punishments or other unpleasant sensations associated with the object on which it is imprinted. In the years following this discovery much research was carried out on imprinting and it was found that the "early learning in the impressionable phase" was applicable in the most varied contexts.

Some maintain that the attachment of a cat to its owner can be explained by reference to imprinting. According to this theory, in the first months of its life, a cat undergoes a critical period regarding the development of social relationships. During this period (the "sensitive period") it establishes very close links with members of its own species and with man, whether it is treated with affection, aggression or indifference. The "imprinting" of a cat on its future owner, therefore, has nothing to do with his attitude toward the animal.

This theory, although extremely fascinating, leaves some doubt. If it were true for the cat, the sensitive phase would have to be extremely long and flexible, an unusual characteristic for imprinting. We know that in practice cats arrive in the home (whether bought from a pet shop, acquired as a gift, or picked up in the street) at an age between forty-five days and six months (leaving aside the rather rare cases of cats of more than a year old). Because links of affection are generally established without much difficulty (except in the case of abnormal behaviour on the part of the cat or particularly disturbing family situations) it would be necessary to accept that the imprinting period is fairly elastic, although this is as yet neither proven nor disproven.

The functional theory: this is based on the theory of natural selection. Since to have an owner means the assurance of food and shelter, it is possible that when the process of domestication began (about five thousand years ago) the tendency to establish affective links with a human being was naturally selected by cats. Those cats that did attach themselves to an owner showed distinct advantages: for example, they were seen to reproduce better than those that did not develop this relationship.

It is important to bear in mind that we are speaking of a selective process aimed mainly at the development of an affective attachment to an owner, without identify-

The whiskers

In cats the whiskers, the correct name for which is *"vibrissae,"* are its basic sense organs and not secondary sexual characteristics as in humans. Both males and females have them: they are rooted into the skin on the cheeks and stick out appreciably on either side of the cat's face. They are extremely sensitive to contact and are a warning system to cats of the proximity of objects. If they are lightly touched the eyes instantly close and, in complete darkness, the cat can still be aware of any obstacle.

The eyes

Cats' eyes present two characteristics that make these predators capable of hunting when there is scarcely any light, an indispensible exercise for survival in their original wild habitat. The iris (the contractile circular coloured membrane with a circular black opening in the center) has muscles which make the pupil (the opening) dilate or contract according to the amount of light to which it is exposed. In full sunlight the pupil is reduced to a vertical slit; with very little light it is enlarged until it obliterates the iris almost entirely, becoming a full circle; in this way it makes the most of the slightest ray of light. Cats' eyes have an inner cellular covering able to reflect and amplify any light from outside. This is why their eyes are called "phosphorescent" (a characteristic of many other predators such as the hyena), and a fact which contributed to the belief during the Middle Ages that the cat was a creature of the devil.

The paws

A cat's paws are highly functional. The pads act as tactile organs because they are able to pick up vibrations from the ground. At the same time, they are responsible for the cat's characteristically quiet, soft tread, which allows it to surprise its prey, or to flee from its own predators. The other basic parts are the claws, which are only evident if one lightly presses the paw between two fingers. They are held in the recessive sheaths between the pads and are unsheathed only for defense or attack. They are essential for escape because they allow the cat to climb quickly. *Never* try to trim them yourself.

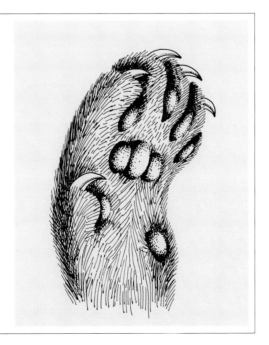

ing the owner as the provider of food. In proof of this, studies carried out by a group of researchers in animal behaviour at the university of Zurich on the effects that provision of food may have on cat-man relationships demonstrated that the preference of a cat for a human being is unrelated to who is feeding it. More precisely, it was seen that the regular provision of food may influence the initial phases of relating to members of the family, causing the cat to prefer the one giving the meals; later, however, it was observed that the cat would choose as its owner even someone who had never fed it. In practice, dependence for food is not identified with the affective link.

Given then that the functional theory maintains that the selection process could have caused the evolution of the affective link with the owner independently of whether he or she provides food, let us examine the doubts raised by this hypothesis. Five thousand years (the period between the beginning of domestication to the present day) is a short time to select so complex a relationship as that which links a cat to a human being, particularly as natural selection could not have developed at the same pace in all parts of the world.

In the past, feline populations lived in or near areas colonized by man, but many others had no contact at all with the human species. We therefore need to think in terms of a discontinuous selective process, or else attach great importance to the extreme behavioural flexibility of the cat that has made possible the evolution of such a complex phenomenon in a shorter time than could have been expected.

The theory of the social companion: it has been observed that a cat can develop a deep and lasting relationship with a human being that it will never form with another cat. Nor is this kind of relationship ever found between adult individuals of the same social group, whether they are female or, even less likely, male.

More surprising still, even felines with a more solitary life-style than the domestic cat, such as the ocelot, are able to establish an affective link with man. Paul Leyhausen,

an expert on cat behaviour, believes that in the eyes of the cat a human being may be the ideal social companion, because it does not represent a potential competitor for resources; the tendency to establish a strong social link with its human companion is therefore not inhibited by the aggression inherent in relationships between adult cats. For example, two males belonging to the same social group will tolerate one another in the confines of the group territory, but are not otherwise bound by a friendly relationship. Two male cats that have reached full sexual maturity will never (or rarely) be seen sleeping close to each other. Many male household cats, however, seek regular close contact with their owners.

Leyhausen maintains that the continuous activities of controlling and defending their territory, antagonism to other members of the species, and the mating of cats within a social group leave no room for infantile behaviour for either male or female. The relationship with man, on the contrary,

facilitates displays of friendliness and playfulness, and is a positive encouragement to infantile behaviour. Leyhausen thus suggests that the relationship with man is a social link of the interspecific type.

In conclusion, nothing is yet known for certain about the attachment of a cat to the human being it has chosen. The theories formulated are not necessarily alternatives; in each of them there could be elements of truth, but a great deal of experimental work remains to be done before any kind of definitive explanation can be offered, if indeed this is at all possible.

The rôle of play in the cat's development

The significance of play has always been difficult for students of animal behaviour. Instinctively everyone would define it as "a range of activities which serves to amuse, helps one to think of nothing, and to relax." For the human species play undoubtedly has all these attributes. But what about all the many other species that play?

The instinct to play is present in all vertebrates but absent in fish, amphibians, reptiles and invertebrates and so appears to be linked to a certain development of the brain. The more evolved the species the more likely it is to manifest the tendency to play. Man, indeed, plays throughout his life, frequently turning game-playing into a career, as with sport, for example. It is important to make a distinction between "exploration" and "play": to explore means to make contact and thus become familiar with new objects and surroundings; to play means to use objects and surroundings in new ways. Having finished exploring, an animal or a man will stop wondering what the new object is and begin to ask himself what game he can play with it. According to researchers of animal behaviour, the behavioural category of "play" includes the separate and distinct activities of manipulation of objects without apparent purpose, which implies experimentation, exploration, learning and control of the animal's own body, his surroundings and the other living beings which inhabit them.

With regard to the rôle of play in the development of the cat, it would seem, although it is difficult to prove scientifically, that playful activities are by no means gratuitous. The theories that have been put forward suggest that the impulse to play pushes the kitten toward learning in advance what is the correct behaviour to apply in its adult life. The playful kitten "fighting" with its little siblings learns movements that will be used aggressively over matters of territory or of predominance typical of adulthood; it plays with a ball of wool or the end of a piece of string drawn across the floor, putting into practice the movements of hunting, in other words it is experimenting, trying out the behaviour which will enable it to survive as an adult.

These theories have been criticized with the argument that play is too wasteful of energy for an animal to be able to allow itself the luxury of engaging for the greater part of its infancy in an activity demanding great effort for no immediate gain. However, it is significant that behaviour patterns did evolve in the wild, where kittens played without having secured their food.

A further argument is that during play the animal is distracted and thus vulnerable to attack by predators, but a recent study on

the expenditure of energy in the cat during play has shown, surprisingly, that the daily energy output is very low, between 4% and 9% of the total output (excluding the energy spent on bodily growth).

Thus, at least in the cat, it would seem that play does not involve an expenditure of energy that must be justified by important short-term benefits. Nevertheless, the benefits are conspicuous, even if they are difficult to measure. Play is not a simple medley of infantile behaviour, but an extremely complex phenomenon, because it is very free and variable, and not constrained by rigid, stereotyped patterns. Play introduces novelty into the behaviour, continuously providing the individual with opportunities to learn and increase its potential for adapting to its surroundings. In its most effective manifestations it has led the most highly-evolved species (man in particular, but also certain kinds of monkey) to discoveries that have been culturally transmitted. This is not yet the case with the cat, though it is beyond doubt that through its play it learns to survive.

Behaviour during oestrus

This section deals with females because, as is the case with many other mammals, it is only the females that have well-defined periods during which they are fertile, and available for mating. These periods (in the case of cats five to six days) are called "oestrus." Like the wildcat, queens originally had one or two periods of oestrus each year between spring and summer, so that the young would be born when the weather was milder, and prey more abundant. Gestation lasted sixty-two to sixty-five days, as it still does. Cats living indoors no longer have to face these problems, because of cental heating and the constant availability of food, and have consequently undergone physical changes. In a single year there may be an indefinite number of oestral periods. This may also be due to the fact that if a female does not become pregnant during oestrus, she will again be on heat fifteen to twenty days later. In the wild this mechanism served to give a second chance to a female which, for whatever reason, did not become pregnant at the first mating. It is another example of a physiological mechanism maintained by cats even though it is no longer an advantage to them in their present environment.

Males have no oestrus, and are ready for mating all the year round. One can be misled by the behaviour of a cat that lives permanently indoors with no possibility of mating, and at certain periods of the year mews more than usual, demanding to be let out. He is not on heat: it may be that he is showing a greater need for mating because it is spring, the period when male mammals in general are more restless and females have their first oestrus, or because he has perceived the mewings or the scent of a female on heat living nearby. A female not on heat shows no interest in mating (she is not fertile, so it would make no sense), and reacts most aggressively to male approaches.

As we have seen, a female rarely sprays urine, but if this happens she is almost certainly on heat. In this case the purpose of such behaviour is not territory-marking,

but to attract males. The urine of a female on heat contains certain substances (pheromones) that are different from those in the urine sprayed by a male. Female pheromones carry chemical messages announcing the fertile condition of the queen, and her availability for mating. By spreading these messages around through her urine a queen is trying to attract the tomcats in the vicinity. Even urine emitted in the normal, crouching position when a cat is on heat may contain pheromones. A cat on heat may be noticed urinating more often than usual in the litter tray. This is another way of spreading chemical messages. In fact, a household cat of extremely clean habits may sometimes surprise its owner by urinating outside the litter tray during oestrus. This anomalous behaviour will disappear at the end of the period of heat, because she will then feel no further urge to send such messages. All the other displays that are related to this period, such as persistent

mewing, rolling on the ground, arching of the back, and bending of the legs, will also disappear.

The actions described above, which are characteristic of a female during oestrus, can be tiresome for the inhabitants of the house. However, we must remember that it is limited to a few days, and that for the rest of the time females are very quiet and clean.

For anyone who has the time to devote to the cat, the best solution is to mate her and follow her progress through the absorbing experience of pregnancy, birth, and the raising of the kittens. Otherwise, various other steps can be taken. For a female living in an apartment with no possibility of mating, spaying is the best solution. The cat will not suffer in the slightest. On the contrary, she may prove to be more peaceful and able to develop her gifts of intelligence, vivacity and playfulness without problems. In fact, it is as well to remember that every oestrus

passed without mating can cause considerable psycho-physical stress for a cat.

If instead you live in the country and your cat has freedom of movement, another kind of operation may be performed. The vet can surgically tie the fallopian tubes so that, while still going into heat, a queen can mate freely without the risk of becoming pregnant.

The third solution is the administration of drugs (either orally or by injection) at the first signs of oestrus. The symptoms should disappear and the cat will not become pregnant. Unfortunately, there are still uncertainties regarding the prevention of pregnancy by drugs; the long-term effects of drugs used as contraceptives are not yet known, and there is a suspicion that they may cause cancer. The recommendations of a vet are in any case essential for the programming of the right treatment for your particular cat.

In conclusion, there is one thing that is absolutely inadvisable: do not leave anything to chance. If you want your cat to have kittens, there are no problems; but if you are sure that they will be unwelcome take steps to avoid the pregnancy. If she should escape from your control, never act out of desperation by drowning the kittens or abandoning them in the street as soon as they are born: if you cannot find homes for them, take them to a vet, who will put them to sleep painlessly. But it is obviously better to avoid reaching this point. A pet should be a source of joy, not of tension.

Ownerless
cats

The social behaviour of the domestic cat

We have seen how the cat has evolved from a wild to a domesticated animal. The domestication of the cat, principally by management of the mating process, has produced a multitude of colours and kinds of coat, increasing the potential of variability contained in the genotype of the wildcat.

The history of *Felis catus* does not end where domestication began, however. At some point during the establishment of domestication the cat reverted to exercising its own free will in its movements and matings, spurning its owner and returning to the streets. It is impossible to establish when this tendency first began to happen, because it may have been a parallel process to domestication; some cats, while living around human habitations, and accepting food from them, may have fled after the beginning of man's attempts to control their mating.

Many cats have returned to the streets after having lived with an owner either of their own free will or because they have been abandoned. Young males, for example, undergo a phase in which they tend to wander, either as a mechanism which serves to prevent mating between blood relations or because they are chased away by other resident males.

The cat is therefore an extremely interesting subject for the study of evolution of behaviour: it is the product of artificial selection subjected once again to natural selection. The peculiarity of such a phenomenon must have consequences, the most important of which is the acquisition of a high degree of flexibility of behaviour which, from an evolutive standpoint represents an undoubted advantage. The cat is able to adapt to many different environments and thus to colonize them. It is not by chance, for example, that its distribution extends all over the world.

Ownerless cats manage to survive regardless almost of where they are abandoned, feeding on whatever is available; in rural surroundings, they will feed off the prey they have caught, and on food pro-

146

City cats feeding on food remains found in the street.

The adaptive capacity of cats

It is not true that all cats like fish. Contrary to popular belief, fish became part of the feline diet much later than meat, and, surprisingly perhaps, cats do not necessarily find its taste agreeable.

The wildcat lived in environments where it had no contact with fish as prey, but the domestic cat, thanks to its behavioural versatility, has not neglected the sea shores in its conquest of new habitats. Large and small populations of domestic felines live in countries bordering the sea, and are fed principally on fish by the local inhabitants. Studies carried out in Japan bear witness to this theory.

Fishermen returning from the sea with their catch often have in their nets small fish that are unsuitable for the market. The cats wait on the jetty, or on the shore. While unloading their boats the men throw the small fish that are left over, still alive, to the waiting cats. The cats, often fighting among themselves, seize their free meal, and run off to devour it in a secluded corner where they will not be disturbed.

Some domestic cats, therefore, like raw fish, but by no means all. Some of those not living in a coastal environment, may reject it in preference to meat; others cannot digest it, and may regurgitate it. Cats reared in houses, less hardy, must be fed cooked fish, with all the bones carefully removed. The reason is that some fish contains substances that are harmful to the cat's system, but that are eliminated during cooking.

However, let us not forget the cat's great capacity for adaptation: in environments where the principal food resource is raw fish, cats may not only have developed a preference for the taste of this food, but also the physical tolerance of it. It has been demonstrated experimentally that the wildcat dislikes fish: a wildcat raised in captivity and placed in front of such food will sniff it curiously and at length, then take no further interest. It does not recognize it and will not eat it.

vided by farmers; in urban surroundings, where they do not hunt, they will rummage among the rubbish, or may find food left for them by cat lovers. Predators or scavengers, cats will always exploit the resources of the environment in which they find themselves.

Some experts on animal behaviour have described the domestic cat as a solitary animal, like its progenitor, the wildcat, which will have contact with other members of its species only during mating. Other studies, in contrast, have demonstrated the cat's capacity to live in very large social groups. It was found that the researchers described the cat as solitary or social depending on where they were carrying out their studies, proving that the domestic cat has different life-styles in different habitats.

This makes the study of the cat's evolution more interesting still, because the comparison between different social groupings of the same species, living in different places but at the same time, reveals such a degree of adaptability.

The domestic cat is an animal of great behavioural flexibility, able to adapt to many kinds of habitat. It is even found in coastal environments, where it lives on fish. Its progenitor, the wildcat *(Felis sylvestris)*, will not, however, accept such food.

Colonized habitats

There are cats that live in the streets, in the countryside and on islands. Their common denominator is that they have no owner. In other words, although most of them receive food provided by humans, they have no direct relationship with an owner, and very few are domesticated to the extent that they can be approached and treated affectionately.

Studies have been made on cats living on certain sub-Antarctic islands (Kerguelen, Marion Island, Macquarie, and the Ile aux Cochons, which is one of the Crozet Islands) because they are true examples of domestic cats having reverted to the wild state. They were taken to these deserted islands by men who remained briefly and left them there on their departure. In spite of the cold climate and the difficulty of finding food, the cats survived and reproduced. They now live by hunting, and are organized very similarly to the wildcat, that is, they are solitary and territorial, and their population density is low (from two to twenty per km^2).

Cats also live in the vicinity of rural settlements. They receive a certain amount of food from the occupants of farms in the area. This not being always sufficient, they supplement their diet by hunting. The population density is higher in this case than in the preceding example (over twenty cats per km^2). The organization of groups is also different. Let us look at a group living around a farm: the territory of each cat tends to overlap and, although the existence of an area preferred by each cat may be noted, it is more correct to speak in terms of a single common territory, which is defended collectively against the intrusion of strangers of the same species. Contacts between the cats are frequent and the group presents a certain internal organization.

Studies on rural cats have been conducted in Britain, Switzerland, France and Australia: the differences found in social organization are sufficient to indicate that, as a general rule, rural cats group together in a more conspicuous manner than those that have colonized the sub-Antarctic

Even in the midst of city traffic cats can find a space to live.

City cats: urban grouping

islands, but more loosely than those living in cities.

The most striking cat groupings are found in the urban environment. Certain cities are famous for this phenomenon. What visitor can fail to have been impressed by the large number of cats that populate the historic centers of Rome, Paris, London or Venice, for example?

Cats will colonize whatever space is available, whether it is the ruins of ancient monuments, public or private gardens, courtyards, or simply blind alleys. Nowhere is too grand, and nowhere too humble.

F igures relating to the population density for cats may seem surprisingly high – over 200 cats per km². Naturally, this does not mean that there are 200 cats for *every* square kilometer, but that in city areas where they are most concentrated such figures have been recorded.

Research on this subject has been carried out in Britain, Italy and Japan, with fairly similar results. The cats live in groups that reside permanently in one particular place. Such areas, varying in size, have very precise boundaries which are defended by all

the members of the group. If a strange cat, male or female, enters the protected area (not an infrequent occurrence, since many groups live in neighbouring areas) it is immediately attacked by the occupants, sometimes even by two or three cats at the same time. This action is performed by adults against other adults: the young do not involve themselves in the defense of the territory (although they will show curiosity when they encounter strangers), and any young, unknown cats that introduce themselves into a group do not generally provoke aggressive reactions. This is probably due to the physical and behavioural characteristics of the young animals, which tend to inhibit the aggressiveness of their adults.

To discover whether groups of cats change their composition frequently or maintain a certain stability, daily observations of the members of groups have been made over a period of at least one year (and in some cases two or three). These studies served the purpose of checking how many and which cats were present within the protected area at a given time.

The results obtained have established that the city cat is a truly territorial animal, relating itself firmly to one territory in particular, to which it returns after its wanderings. This means that groups are always composed of the same individuals.

The argument applies to adult cats that are already part of a group; it is not valid for young males, which tend to leave their place of origin on reaching full physical and sexual maturity. This tendency does not manifest itself in all cases, but it is nevertheless fairly frequent. It may be a mechanism designed to avoid mating with close relations (in technical terms, inbreeding), or it may be that the departure of the young cat is provoked by the male adults, because the former represents a potential new competitor to the latter.

In conclusion, groups of cats living in the city are not floating populations, casually coming together and then dispersing randomly; each group has a very precisely determined configuration.

Above: kittens living in the street choose safe places to sleep, difficult for humans and other animals to reach.

Top: high-ranking male: in addition to physical characteristics such as the large face and robust build, the posture of the ostentatiously erect body also proclaims this cat's hierarchical position in the group.

Sources of food

he city cat's sources of food are rather unusual for an animal which, after all, lives in freedom.

It is an accepted fact that in order to eat the city cat is largely dependent on man. It is true that it also feeds on food waste left in dustbins outside homes, restaurants or hotels, but this is of insufficient quantity to nourish it adequately. These cats do not hunt: city rats are too large and aggressive to be normal prey; sparrows and pigeons would be suitable, but city cats tend to become lazy, and prey upon them more as a result of inherited instinct and for sport than out of necessity. The reason for this is because every day they are brought considerable quantities of food by many people who regularly visit the places where feline colonies are established. Food is always abundant, and usually of reasonable quality. Each feline population has its regular suppliers who never fail to arrive; they are many and devoted; consequently the food is distributed at various times throughout the day.

For these dedicated cat lovers caring for such cats provides an interesting change from their humdrum daily routine, and for many of them it is nothing short of a reason for living. Not only do these people take food to the cats, but they even make shelters for them, and often care for the animals when they are sick.

The number of cats in a colony is related to the amount of food available. In 1979, for example, the number of cats living in the Belvedere Tarpeo park in the center of Rome, was about thirty. The food cat lovers took there was sufficient but not over-abundant, and it was regularly eaten up by the animals. In 1986 the feline population living in an enclosed area of Rome's Piazza Vittorio Emanuele, consisted of about eighty individuals. The size of this second territory was smaller than the Belvedere Tarpeo park, but the cats that had colonized it were more than double in number. They were, however, receiving such an excessive amount of food that often it was wasted.

A box-shelter made by a cat lover who takes care of the group to which this white cat belongs.

When crowding around the person bringing them food, cats hold their tails high. This typical infantile behaviour when receiving food from the mother is retained in the adult as a display of friendly intentions.

Social organization

Students of feline behaviour have theorized that the formation of social groups originally arose from the tendency to gravitate toward a source of food. While this is true, it is not the only reason, otherwise the groups would be transient, and after feeding, the cats would disperse until they met the next day. Instead, they form stable groups within which certain cats recognize each other individually by sight and smell. In addition to feeding, they develop many daily activities in the same communal territory: sleeping, playing, courting, mating, fighting, and rearing their kittens. These groups are made up of male and female adults (over eighteen months old), male and female sub-adults (between one year and eighteen months), young males and females (between six months and one year), and kittens of both sexes (younger than six months). The meetings and contacts between group members are very frequent. It could hardly be otherwise since, although the numbers in the groups vary greatly, there is always a large number of animals concentrated in a restricted area. Scientific papers have mentioned groups of ten, thirty, and eighty individuals.

Sexual dimorphism (the difference between male and female) is not obvious at first glance: with a little training, however, it is easily possible to distinguish between the members of the two sexes. Male adults are solid with rather square heads, holding their tails in a typically arched position and walking in a prancing manner. The females are smaller and have more rounded or triangular noses.

In most feline groups there is usually one dominant male for which other males make way if they do not actually flee. He has the first pick of the food and marks the territory by leaving traces of his own scent through his urine or other secretions.

Below this leader there is no clearly defined hierarchy. Broadly speaking, there are males of high and low standing. These also show territorial behaviour in marking territory and are the most colourful individuals in the group: large in size, strong, and

Playful behaviour between an adult and a young cat belonging to the same social group.

Male adult cats of equal status sometimes fight ferociously. Real clashes (as opposed to ritual combats) are bloody and the animals often inflict injuries on each other. In the photograph above the scars of wounds from earlier fights are visible on the ears of the cat facing the camera.

"dramatic" in all their actions. Real fighting is rare; most of the time they engage in ritualistic combat with much noise and little action. They confront each other with rigid legs, bristling fur, ears held back and at the moment of maximum tension emit shrill cries. Eventually one of the two gives in, and gradually withdraws, without running away, however, as this would provoke immediate chase.

The victor's behaviour varies: generally he remains in a threatening position for several minutes, ostentatiously swallowing the saliva that has accumulated during the excitement; this is followed by territory marking with his urine. He may roll about on the ground full of self-satisfaction and conceit or rub his chin against the objects nearest the battlefield in order to leave the scent of the glandular secretions from behind his jaw. Ritualistic combats are more frequent than real fights: when real fights occur they are never between an individual of low status and another of a higher rank, nor between a resident cat and a stranger, nor between a tom and a queen. Invariably the combatants are animals of similar size, strength and age. If not, the cat which is the leader on any of these counts will move away and avoid the contest. When the fight takes place it is very bloody: the animals attack each other, biting and clawing, making a single confused mass in which it is hard to tell one cat from the other. The battle lasts a few minutes (sometimes only seconds) and always ends with the speedy flight of the loser pursued by the victor, sometimes for several hundred yards. The entire incident is accompanied by piercing howls. The signs of battle are visible in the scarred ears and muzzles of adult cats. When confronted by an aggressive female, however, any adult male will withdraw.

A peculiarity of the domestic cat is that its behavioural repertoire does not include poses of submission or pacifying actions which, in many other animal species, are present to inhibit the contender's aggression. A frightened cat will crouch, and with its ears flattened, and tail wound round its

The amicable relationship between adult female cats is seen in the way they wash each other.

body, hiss at the cat threatening it. Thus, attitudes signifying the reverse of menace, such as occur with dogs, are not found (Darwin was the first to prove the "principle of antithesis" in the dog), nor other pacifying behaviour as seen in many types of monkey. If the disadvantaged cat has no possibility of flight he will not offer the victor the most vulnerable part of his body, an act which in the wolf, for example, inhibits a mortal blow from the enemy; on the contrary, the cat will fling himself on his back to display to the maximum his weaponry, the

impressive claws on all four paws.

Male adults in a social group do not show signs of friendliness, but rather of tolerance toward each other within the confines of the group territory. It is very rare to see two adult males sleeping in close proximity, and reciprocal recognition is made on a sensory and olfactory basis without either cat coming too close to the other.

This is not the case between adult females or between adults of different sexes. The queens with their kittens, which represent the basic unit of the social group, live

peacefully in the same territory and sleep close to each other at times. Often the females will demonstrate reciprocal signs of friendship, such as nose-to-nose contacts, serving to effect recognition between individuals, and taking place with tails held high; they rub against each other with their bodies and sometimes lick one another. The erect tail is a sign of a friendly attitude, and is an example of infantile behaviour which persists in the adult. Furthermore, many adult females tend to rear their kittens collectively.

There is often mutual sniffing between adult males and females but it is rare for them to have any real physical contact outside mating. Their relationships are, however, amicable, with the male giving way in cases of conflict.

In their confrontations with adults, young individuals of both sexes behave in a concilatory way, thus helping to prevent any aggressive reaction. In encounters between young and adult cats, the young ostentatiously raise their tails and, if they are a short distance away, will approach the adult. They then attempt to rub against the adult, wrapping the tail around the other's body (as they would with an owner). If the adult sniffs the genitals the young cat will remain still for a brief time, permitting the action. This is probably to indicate the

In the domestic cat there is no distinction between youthful and adult livery, unlike other animal species (penguins, seals, gulls).

Two members of the same social group (here, a female and a male adult) recognize each other individually by means of smell during nose-to-nose contact. Their friendly attitude is indicated by the position of their tails, held upright.

youth of the individual to the other adult members of the group, and compensates for the lack of distinction between the youthful and the adult livery shown by many animal species.

Cats develop sexually at about one year old: sub-adults are consequently already able to mate. In fact, females can give birth to their first litter, sometimes only one kitten, in the reproductive season following their birth, around the time that the first attempts of the sub-adult male at courting and mating are shown. The latter thus become new rivals for the adult males which understand these changes in behaviour and smell in the sub-adults, and react aggressively toward them, even causing some of them to move away from the group.

Marking territories

The domestic cat produces two kinds of urine: firstly, there is that sprayed from a standing position, when the cat has its back turned to an object – usually a wall, fence or tree – then, lifting the tail, it directs the spray at the object, in the opposite direction to that in which the head is turned. In this case the urine is not covered with earth or other matter. Secondly, there is the urine deposited on the ground from a crouched position, which is then carefully buried by the animal. The sprayed urine contains pheromones, which are used to mark the territory, while that passed from a crouching position does not contain these chemical substances.

Studies on the reactions of cats to the two kinds of urine have shown that both males and females linger much longer to examine sprayed urine than that which is simply passed to relieve the bladder.

It has also been observed that cats in a community are able to differentiate between the scent of urine sprayed by an outside cat and that sprayed by one belonging to the group, even in the absence of the cat that has left it. They linger much longer over traces of a strange cat, analyzing them carefully. To do this, they use a special receptor known as Jacobson's organ, a structure in the roof of the mouth found also in horses, cattle, deer, the big cats, and other animals, which serves for the minute analysis of tiny particles of an inhaled compound. This organ gives cats an extra sense which is halfway between taste and smell.

During this operation cats demonstrate a behavioural sequence known as "flehming." After placing the nose in contact with the substance they raise the head and hold it stiffly upward; the mouth is half-open, the nostrils dilated, the eyes expressionless, the breathing slow and deep. Flehming lasts from a few seconds to several minutes.

Chemical communication plays an important rôle in the social group. The dominant male marks with his urine more than any other member of the group, but other high-ranking males have also been observed to do so extensively. Females spray rarely, and mostly when they are on heat, their urine containing the pheromones which serve to attract the males.

Sub-adult males, unlike young males which do not manifest marking behaviour, occasionally spray their urine. Together with other behaviour, the act proclaims the reaching of adulthood.

Low-ranking males mark little or not at all. According to an interesting, but scientifically unproven theory, the odour of the pheromones contained in the urine of the dominant male may inhibit certain behaviour in other males, including marking. It is a form of indirect competition.

It may seem difficult to believe that smell should have such power, but we must not forget that olfactory communication is much more highly developed in animals than in man. We should not underestimate its effect: in rats it has been demonstrated that contact with the urine of a strange male by a pregnant female, even in his absence, can cause reabsorption of the foetus (a phenomenon known as "the Bruce effect").

Another method of territorial marking used by the cat is rubbing the chin (beneath which are located certain sebaceous glands) against objects in the surroundings to leave its scent on them.

It is debatable whether the action of scratching tree trunks with the claws is of significance in territory marking; it is much more probable that this serves to remove the old outer layer of the claws. Cats frequently demonstrate this behaviour, but in an irregular fashion.

With the possible exception of marking territory by means of urine, all other behaviour characteristics are exhibited by females as well as males.

The behaviour of territory marking by means of sprayed urine is manifested principally by adult males. They turn their back on the object and spray it with small quantities of urine containing substances (pheromones) which serve to communicate certain information to other members of the species (both male and female).

Reproductive behaviour

It is natural to assume that the dominant tomcat in a group would, as in many other species, have priority of access to the female, but this is not always the case. For some as yet unexplained reason the male cats in a group court a female on heat together, following her around for days, and mating with her without any pre-established order. The actual preamble to copulation, during which the female sits in wait for her preferred first mate, can be quite lengthy, in stark contrast to the act itself which can be as brief as a few seconds.

In the domestic cat courting does not follow a particular and stereotyped behavioural sequence; it consists of the male following a female around for long periods, trying from time to time to mate with her, when she is demonstrating encouragement and is in a sexually responsive mood. Several males (from two to ten) act in this way simultaneously, surrounding her, like a court of suitors, or following her and even pursuing her if she flees.

The queen often takes up a higher position (on a tree, a rock, a dustbin or a wall) and awaits their courting from a good visual vantage point. When she is ready to mate, one of them moves slowly toward her, advancing sometimes just a few steps at a time, "freezing," then finally getting close enough to mount her back and mate with her, holding her steady by grasping the scruff of her neck between his teeth.

The others wait, sometimes calmly, at times in a state of considerable agitation. When they can no longer restrain themselves, they intervene and disturb the tom which is mating, bite the female on the side of the neck, or try to get in between the two; some of them may actually climb on top of the male, creating a small pyramid of cats. Amazingly, the disturbed cat does not react in a particularly aggressive manner to this disturbance. Indeed, not even during the waiting period are the males very aggressive to one another, although the whole scene may be punctuated by bouts of caterwauling and snarling. And such outbursts

are certainly not enough to send the lower-ranking cats packing; their concentration on the female seems to be so intense that what goes on around them does not present a great distraction.

During oestrus period (average duration five to six days), the females mate with numerous males. Although they do not ovulate until after the first mating, the fact that they indulge in multiple-partner activity throughout the oestrus period means that any one of the males may be the sire of the future offspring. The litter could even have more than one father, although this has not been scientifically proved. Multiple paternity could occur following competition of the sperm of several individuals introduced into the female genital tract, and of successive fertilizations of eggs during the same period of fertility.

If the theory is correct, mating with a number of males could be good strategy for the female, increasing the genetic variability of her offspring. But if it is advantageous for the female it may not be so for the indi-

Above: when a male mates, the other individuals courting the same female arrange themselves around the couple and wait their turn.

Below: disturbing action on the part of a male against two mating cats is fairly common. Surprisingly, in most cases it is tolerated, and does not provoke an aggressive reaction in the disturbed male.

Opposite: during oestrus a female is courted by numerous males, which follow her around. Among the males, there is not a high level of aggression and they tolerate one another even at close quarters. The most important objective is to get as close as possible to the female (in the photograph this is the grey tabby sitting on the end of the ladder, next to the ginger male).

vidual male. Why, then, does the dominant male spend time and energy in territorial behaviour, exposing himself to the risk of injury in battle if there is no corresponding monopolization of the female to assure himself of a larger number of offspring than any other male? One possible explanation may be that the female, as has been established for other species, attains a peak of fertility during oestrus, and that this is the moment the dominant male monopolizes: the physical change might be signalled by a change of scent perceptible to animals.

In the eyes of a human observer, all the males seem to mate casually and in equal measure, but this may not necessarily be the case. By securing for himself the female's moment of maximum fertility, the dominant male would be able to leave the field open to the others after he had staked his claim.

There is a further theory, to explain which we must go back to the origins of the domestic cat. The wildcat lives as a solitary animal, and his territory often includes some females, but not other males, so that in a sexual contest the contenders for a female on heat are rarely more than two.

In a confrontation with a single individual, mere aggression can be enough to settle the issue. The domestic cat in a similar situation, on the other hand, finds himself confronted with an indefinite number of adversaries. Because the ability to organize into social groups is a recent development arising from a rapid change of environment, it may be that behavioural mechanisms have not yet been sufficiently evolved to deal with the problem posed by this new situation: how to stand up to five or six males at once and mate with the female.

While a cat is engaged in direct battle with another, any one of the waiting males could take advantage of the fact that his attention has been diverted from the female to succeed in mating with her.

After mating, males take no further interest in the female, and none in the future offspring. In fact, they tend to show toward kittens an attitude which is both curious and timid. If an adult male happens to come

across a newly-born litter when the female is not present, it will sniff at the kittens for a long time; his attitude remaining circumspect, perhaps because of possible aggressive reactions from the mother. If the kittens are older and try to take a few paces toward the adult there may be a reaction of irritation on his part (often the male gives a few light taps of the paw to the kitten, without, however, wounding it) after which he retires rapidly.

True to his reputation, the cat remains typically detached, and unemotional as ever.

Below: during the kittens' weaning period an urban mother is more likely to show the hunting instinct, generally dormant in city cats. She wants to teach the kittens to eat solid food.

Raising the kittens

Bringing up the kittens is the sole responsibility of the mother, with no help from the father. Some time after the birth several mothers often put their litters together and rear the kittens collectively. The "nursery" area in which this takes place is usually in the safest part of the territory, far from its boundaries, and full of hiding places. The mother cats bring their own offspring (or, if they are old enough, the kittens follow the mother there), and the mothers then take turns in looking after them, feeding, washing, protecting them, and playing with them, whether they are their own young or not.

A female cat will initially accept kittens other than her own, but as she grows more familiar with the kittens from her own litter she will favour those. Later, when her kittens are older, she will accept other kittens more readily, and this is when the phenomenon of collective raising is seen in groups of cats.

After a while the cats no longer discriminate between their own kittens and the others, or at least this is the impression they give to an observer. Possibly they distinguish their own young on the basis of some unseen characteristic, such as smell for example. In some cases the cats show preferential behaviour toward their own kittens while allowing the others close proximity.

A necessary prerequisite for this phenomenon of collective raising, which in general is very widespread, is the predisposition of the female cats to adopt no matter which kitten. The cooperative upbringing has a precise functional significance for city cats: the combined action of several cats provides a more suitable atmosphere for the kittens' development than that of a solitary cat. The kittens' mental faculties develop better because they grow in a social climate full of stimuli afforded, among other things, by the continuous games of their many adoptive siblings (in a single collective group there can be as many as forty kittens).

There are obviously some disadvantages, for example the fact that kittens of different ages are brought up together and must compete for the acquisition of the teat: the smallest often have no chance of winning. Cats have been seen simultaneously suckling kittens from a week old to one month.

Group life can spread certain illnesses (which are not contagious to man). For example, Feline Viral Rhinotracheitis (FVRV: a form of cat 'flu) claims many victims, especially kittens. Being a respiratory infection (which produces the same symptoms as a cold: coughs and mucus from the nose and eyes) it is spread by kittens sleeping in close contact with each other. Very often the kittens become blind and die – the mortality rate is high – or sometimes they lose an eye.

Why do cats gather and live in social groups?

There is no precise answer as to what extent the domestic cat may be regarded as a social animal. There are qualities which could cause it to be described as an animal inclined to form complex social groups, but it certainly does not attain the organizational levels of groups found in some species of monkey, for example.

It is interesting to note that there is no clearly defined hierarchy among adult tomcats under the leader, and even he is not always necessarily the one with priority of access to resources; besides, in the domestic cat's behavioural repertoire certain stereotyped sequences are missing (defensive attitudes, pacifying actions), that are basic for communication between members of the same social group. One certain fact is that all the members of a group know each other.

So it would be more accurate to say that in certain environments *Felis catus* is an animal still undergoing a process of transformation. It is naturally impossible to predict the final result of this change, even if the direction taken is clearly toward sociability.

Ecological pressures generally thought to be responsible for the formation of social groups in carnivores, have been of two kinds: the need in animals to form a hunting group in order to catch larger prey, as with wolves; and the need to ensure self-defense against other predators in order to save lives but also, as in the case of hyenas, to prevent dead prey from being stolen by more powerful predators.

The first of these two ecological factors could also have been the reason behind the creating of social groups in lions which, as has been seen, have devised systems of group-hunting packs. This does not explain with any certainty why the domestic cat should have given up the solitary way of life, typical of its ancestor the wildcat, to move toward sociability. In fact the domestic cat lives in groups but hunts alone if it hunts at all.

The benefits of group life in urban surroundings are many; in the first place there is the communal defense of territory, food, and prey. In the city defense of territory against outside cats is far more important than in the country because the space available in towns is more limited than in rural surroundings. Also, cooperation in defending offspring from other predators (which in urban environments includes humans as well as other animals) is a further advantage. Finally, in a social context, there is the opportunity to take advantage of the experience of other group members as in the communal rearing of the kittens (contrary to what is generally believed, animals too need to learn about giving birth and bringing up their own offspring).

Sociability is determined first of all by the availability of food resources. Where they are abundant groups will form but where food is quite scarce, and the sources widely scattered, sociability is less likely. Obviously, for the domestic cat which has colonized its urban surroundings, living as part of a group has advantages over leading a solitary life.

In other environments, such as some sub-Antarctic islands, for example, the cat lives as a solitary animal because the prey which constitutes its only food supply is too small to be divided with others. Consequently, sociability as such is unknown in these conditions.

Females belonging to the same social group tend to bring their kittens together and rear them communally, even if they are of different ages.

Opposite: The kind of colony found among cats in different habitats is related to the availability of food in the area. In cities food provided for the animals by humans is enough for social groups to form.

The pattern by which groups evolve is very simple. The nucleus of the community is formed by the mother cats and their kittens; contrary to the custom of the wildcat, many of the kittens do not disperse during their first year of life. Groups thus result that are made up of closely related individuals, and in which cooperation in bringing up offspring, defense of territory and of food is still more advantageous because the cats adopting such groups are favouring their own kind against outsiders. This so-called "kinship selection" is also found in the lion, the only other feline recognized as social in scientific literature.

"Stray": what does it mean?

L et us briefly consider the well-established but, in many cases, incorrect use of the word "stray." Dictionaries give many definitions: "an animal that wanders alone," "separated from the herd," "ownerless," and so on.

According to some experts, any cat becomes a stray the minute it is around the corner, out of sight of its home. Indeed, well-intentioned people often pick up and take home a cat mewing in the street, assuming – if it has no collar – that it has no owner, and is therefore a stray. Often it will have lost its bearings, having wandered too far from home and will be grateful for some

Keeping numbers down

food and attention. When it shows signs of restlessness it is as well to let it go, or return it to the place where it was found. Fed and rested, it will probably find its way home with little trouble.

Cats whose uncaring owners move house, leaving them behind because "cats can always look after themselves" are not strays. They have been abandoned. Some become feral, not approaching humans and distrusting those people who would take them in. If they are fortunate they may succeed in becoming part of a colony (where they will have little social standing), managing to get enough to eat thanks to regular deliveries of food from cat lovers. Some may eventually die of malnutrition and general debility if they are not strong enough to fight for their share of the food.

Then there are the most unlucky felines: kittens that are given as Christmas presents to children whose parents have no intention of keeping a cat; the kittens are often abandoned after Christmas when the novelty of their presence has worn off. They stand small chance of becoming strays and will most likely be killed on the roads. Some cats will wander into a neighbour's garden and, not being chased away, will return to visit again, becoming bolder each time, moving nearer to the house, and finally approaching the doorstep. If the house-owner gives them food they will eventually enter the house and make themselves at home, returning to their own abode for their regular meals. They may take up residence in their "second" home. In a sense they too are strays. Occasionally, after living for a long time with the adopted owners they leave them and return to their original keepers, quite unaware of the anguish they have caused (and are possibly causing the second household).

Adult toms or males that have been neutered late in life are more likely to wander away from home, seeking unknown adventures, and oblivious to the hardships they will meet. These are the real strays, the tough, self-reliant members of the species – voluntary strays.

To remove an adult male from a group of cats living in the streets and then return him to the group is an act which creates many problems for the victim. The finely balanced equilibrium which governs the relationships of cats living together in groups, based on a language of smells, sounds, and physical attitudes, can be disturbed by changing the situation of a single individual.

An adult male is an animal that has completed his development. Having lived for a long time in a certain community he has acquired his own particular odour (a "group scent"), which is recognized by all the other cats, and is due to their type of food, and communal shelters; he will also have established relationships with other individual cats in the community.

When a cat is set free after being neutered, there is the great danger that the other cats in his group will no longer accept him because the anaesthetic and disinfectant have blotted out his own personal scent and, worse, as a result of the operation the odour of his urine will have changed because neutered cats no longer produce testosterone (the chief male sex hormone secreted by the testes). Quite apart from the psychological stress and trauma the animal has endured as a result of being neutered, his general equilibrium could be affected, causing general disorientation. His entire life has been irreversibly changed from that moment; it is only to be hoped that he will eventually readjust, if his former companions in the group do not attack or even kill him. So the debate remains as lively as ever: is it right and necessary to interfere? Is it true that cats living on the street are a problem, and that their numbers should be controlled? In support of the argument against such action, cats rarely contract diseases that can be caught by man, so that particular charge is no reason for destroying them. The practice of neutering as described above, in order to control the growth of the cat population has already been taken up in London; the long-term results of the experiment are as yet

unknown, and hordes of stray cats still live in the city. Perhaps a better solution would be to have the females spayed (an operation which involves tying their fallopian tubes). They could continue life as normal, mating as usual, but without conceiving. Their general social equilibrium would hardly be affected, certainly not in as serious a way as that of the neutered male, whose social relationships are based on scent which is destroyed by the removal of the testes. The argument against this solution is that neutering is more straightforward than spaying, not to mention cheaper.

Neutering is no problem for very young domestic males with owners, but it is a completely different matter for adult males living on the street. Any campaign to control the number of litters should therefore not be undertaken without consideration as to which is the most effective method, and the most beneficial to the cat.

PRACTICAL GUIDE

Gestation calendar

MATING	BIRTH	MATING	BIRTH	MATING	BIRTH	MATING	BIRTH	MATING	BIRTH	MATING	BIRTH
April	June	May	July	June	August	July	September	August	October	September	November
1	5	1	5	1	5	1	4	1	5	1	5
2	6	2	6	2	6	2	5	2	6	2	6
3	7	3	7	3	7	3	6	3	7	3	7
4	8	4	8	4	8	4	7	4	8	4	8
5	9	5	9	5	9	5	8	5	9	5	9
6	10	6	10	6	10	6	9	6	10	6	10
7	11	7	11	7	11	7	10	7	11	7	11
8	12	8	12	8	12	8	11	8	12	8	12
9	13	9	13	9	13	9	12	9	13	9	13
10	14	10	14	10	14	10	13	10	14	10	14
11	15	11	15	11	15	11	14	11	15	11	15
12	16	12	16	12	16	12	15	12	16	12	16
13	17	13	17	13	17	13	16	13	17	13	17
14	18	14	18	14	18	14	17	14	18	14	18
15	19	15	19	15	19	15	18	15	19	15	19
16	20	16	20	16	20	16	19	16	20	16	20
17	21	17	21	17	21	17	20	17	21	17	21
18	22	18	22	18	22	18	21	18	22	18	22
19	23	19	23	19	23	19	22	19	23	19	23
20	24	20	24	20	24	20	23	20	24	20	24
21	25	21	25	21	25	21	24	21	25	21	25
22	26	22	26	22	26	22	25	22	26	22	26
23	27	23	27	23	27	23	26	23	27	23	27
24	28	24	28	24	28	24	27	24	28	24	28
25	29	25	29	25	29	25	28	25	29	25	29
26	30	26	30	26	30	26	29	26	30	26	30
27	**July** 1	27	31	27	31	27	30	27	31	27	**December** 1
28	2	28	**August** 1	28	**September** 1	28	**October** 1	28	**November** 1	28	2
29	3	29	2	29	2	29	2	29	2	29	3
30	4	30	3	30	3	30	3	30	3	30	4
		31	4			31	4	31	4		

MATING	BIRTH	MATING	BIRTH	MATING	BIRTH
October	December	November	January	December	February
1	5	1	5	1	4
2	6	2	6	2	5
3	7	3	7	3	6
4	8	4	8	4	7
5	9	5	9	5	8
6	10	6	10	6	9
7	11	7	11	7	10
8	12	8	12	8	11
9	13	9	13	9	12
10	14	10	14	10	13
11	15	11	15	11	14
12	16	12	16	12	15
13	17	13	17	13	16
14	18	14	18	14	17
15	19	15	19	15	18
16	20	16	20	16	19
17	21	17	21	17	20
18	22	18	22	18	21
19	23	19	23	19	22
20	24	20	24	20	23
21	25	21	25	21	24
22	26	22	26	22	25
23	27	23	27	23	26
24	28	24	28	24	27
25	29	25	29	25	28
26	30	26	30	26	**March** 1
27	31	27	31	27	2
28	**January** 1	28	**February** 1	28	3
29	2	29	2	29	4
30	3	30	3	30	5
31	4			31	6

A cat's normal gestation period is from fifty-six to sixty-five days. For the duration of the pregnancy it is advisable to subdivide the daily food into several meals (five or six) in order to avoid overloading the cat's digestion, to add vitamins, and increase the amount of milk and cheese, which contain calcium.

Fur balls

Cats are extremely clean animals and spend several hours a day licking themselves. In the process they inevitably swallow hair, which can eventually form balls in the stomach. Often the cat manages to vomit the ingested fur, but if not the fur balls can lead to intestinal blockage. Obviously, the problem arises more commonly in longhaired cats. To prevent this it is essential to brush the cat's coat regularly, even daily, and especially at the end of the winter when the moulting season begins.

In the case of obstruction (when the cat is in pain) fresh grass may prove helpful, the ingestion of which helps the cat to get rid of the fur. It is a good idea to keep a pot of grass in the house if you have no garden. This is easily grown from seed. A few teaspoons of liquid paraffin oil given orally from time to time may also help. Always consult your vet if in doubt.

Brushing

It is recommended that you brush your cat's coat regularly, particularly if it is longhaired, but also if it is shorthaired. As well as improving the appearance of the cat's fur, periodic brushing will also reveal any skin infections or parasites. Brushing reduces the amount of hair the cat can swallow and also the amount it can shed around the home. Longhaired cats need brushing daily for five minutes, those with short hair at least once a week. Brushes and combs suitable for the different kinds of coat are sold in all pet shops.

In order to avoid a cat being frightened, and offering resistance, you should get it used to being brushed while it is still small. Brush gently and slowly, but with firm strokes.

Travelling

Cats do not as a rule enjoy travelling. If you must take your cat on a journey, it should be shut in a spacious basket for the duration, preferably with bars so that it can see out. Do not let the cat loose in the car when you are driving. In some countries it is illegal to let a cat out of its basket if there is no passenger to look after it.

To avoid car sickness, the cat may be tranquillized with sedatives, but only on the recommendation of your vet and in a dosage prescribed by him. Cats should not be fed or given any liquid for five to six hours before a journey. Avoid leaving the cat shut up in the car for too long especially in summer; the excessive heat will make it ill or even cause suffocation. If the weather is hot keep a window open a few inches during the journey, but the gap should not be wide enough for the cat to squeeze through. Always remember to take water with you in case the cat needs to drink.

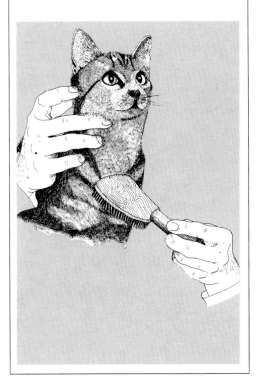

Poisonous substances and plants

TYPE OF POISON	PRODUCTS	IMMEDIATE ACTION	SYMPTOMS
Ethylene glycol	Anti-freeze for cars	Induce vomiting and seek immediate vetinary help	Do not wait for symptoms to appear. Needs immediate care
Organophosphates	Insecticides	On fur: wash with pure soap and seek veterinary advice	Dribbling, muscular spasms, vomiting, diarrhoea, convulsions
Chlorinated hydrocarbons	Insecticides	On fur: wash with pure soap and seek veterinary advice	Dribbling, diarrhoea, hyperactivity, convulsions, muscular spasms
Strychnine	Rat poison ingested by rats or mice themselves	Induce vomiting if the symptoms are not yet apparent	Convulsions, hardening of the muscles, lack of coordination
Metaldehyde	Slug bait	Induce vomiting if the symptoms are not yet apparent	Agitation, shaking, convulsions, vomiting
Salicylates	Aspirin	Unlikely to be eaten spontaneously, avoid administering	Weakness, high temperature, lack of appetite, vomiting, convulsions
Phenol	Disinfectants, antiseptics, weed killers, photographic acids	On fur: wash with soap and water. Ingested: induce vomiting	Listless, shaking, loss of consciousness
Amphetamine	Dietetic pills and stimulants	Induce vomiting and seek veterinary advice	Dilated pupils, delirium, high temperature, convulsions, loss of consciousness
Arsenic	The most widely used poison for rats, ants: weed killers, insecticides	Induce vomiting but care at home ineffective. Seek immediate veterinary help	Digestive upset, blood in diarrhoea, breathing difficulties, collapse, paralysis
Thallium	Modern rat poison	Consult vet at once. Home care ineffective	Vomiting, loss of appetite, sores. Death may occur even two months later
Alkalis	Household cleaning products, grease removers etc.	On fur: wash with soap and water. Ingested: vinegar given orally	Vomiting, abdominal pains
Acids	Preparations for car batteries, metal polishes	On fur: wash with water and apply bicarbonate solution	Vomiting, abdominal pains
Phosphorous	Rat poison, matches, fireworks, tonic medicines, poisoned rat-bait	Ingested: induce vomiting with beaten egg white or salt	Vomiting, blood in diarrhoea, breathing difficulties, collapse, paralysis

Plant	Poisonous parts
Oleander	All foliage
Philodendron	Leaves
Ivy	Leaves and berries
Daphne	Bark, leaves and flowers
Narcissus	Bulbs
Monkshood	All parts
Autumn crocus	All parts
Lilac	Leaves and flowers
Digitalis	Leaves
Dieffenbachia	Leaves

Some house and garden plants can be poisonous to cats.

It is as well to keep watch and if the cat is in the habit of chewing the leaves of a plant, to remove it, or put it out of the cat's reach.

Dieffenbachia (of the Arum family), in particular, can cause irritation of the larynx and temporary paralysis of the vocal chords.

If the cat should ingest any poisonous part of a plant, induce vomiting at once (there are many methods: 2 teaspoons of salt mixed with 4 tablespoons of water, egg white beaten with water, or a teaspoonful of very diluted hydrogen peroxide) and take it to the vet.

Claws

Claws are trimmed only on cats kept exclusively indoors. If it is able to go outside there is no need to for this, because its claws are trimmed when it scratches or climbs trees. Claws should be trimmed with special clippers sold in pet shops.

To perform the operation, open the underside of the paw and press it gently between your fingers. Trim only the tip of the claw, taking special care not to cut into the quick, as this is very painful.

If you do not want to trim the cat's claws yourself, take it to the vet who will do it for you. You could also buy a scratching post on which your cat may "sharpen" its claws itself.

Foreign bodies

If foreign bodies such as thorns, fish bones, bone fragments, or even pins and needles, lodge in the cat's gums or throat, take the cat to the vet at once. The symptoms are that the cat will cough, shake its head, and refuse to eat.

Bathing

Accustom the cat to bathing from kittenhood. Bath the animal in a small basin of lukewarm water; use pure soap. Rinse thoroughly and dry well. Occasional massaging of the coat with commercially available products may be a substitute for bathing.

Bibliography

De Boer, J.N. - 1977 - *The age of olfactory cues functioning in chemocommunication among male domestic cats* - Behav. Processes, 2 (3), 209-225

De Boer, J.N. - 1977 - *Dominance relations in pairs of domestic cats* - Behav. Processes, 2 (3), 227-242

Derenne, P.L. - 1976 - *Notes sur la biologie du chat haret de Kerguelen* - Mammalia 40: 532-595

Izawa, M.; Doi, T. and Ono, X. - 1982 - *Grouping patterns of feral cats (Felis catus) living on a small island in Japan* - Jap. J. Ecol. 32: 373-382

Jones, E. - 1977 - *Ecology of the feral cat, Felis catus L. (Carnivora: Felidae) on Macquarie Island* - Austr. Wildl. Res. 4: 249-262

Barrett, P. and Bateson, P. - 1977 - *The development of play in cats* - Behaviour, 66, 1-2, 106-110

Bertram, B.C.R. - 1975 - *The social system of lions* - Scient. Am. 232: 54-65

Condé, B. and Schauenberg, P. - 1971 - *Le poids du chat forestier d'Europe (Felis silvestris Schreber)* - Revue Suisse de Zoologie 78, issue 2, no. 10: 295-315

Condé, B. and Schauenberg, P. - 1974 - *Reproduction du chat forestier (F. silvestris Sch.) dans le nord-est de la France* - Revue Suisse de Zoologie 81 (1): 45-52

Dards, J.L. - 1983 - *The behaviour of dockyard cats: interactions of adult males* - Applied Animal Ethology 10: 133-153

Packer, C. and Pusey, A.E. - 1983 - *Cooperation and competition in lions* - Nature 302:356

Panaman, R. - 1981 - *Behaviour and ecology of free-ranging female farm cats (Felix catus L.)* -Z. Tierpsychol. 56: 59-73

Ragni, B. - *Gatto selvatico (Felis silvestris Schreber)* - Distribuzione e biologia di 22 specie di mammiferi in Italia, CNR

Schauenberg, P. - 1970 - *Le chat forestier d'Europe Felis silvestris Schreber en Suisse* - Revue Suisse de Zoologie 77, issue 1, no. 8: 127-160

Van Aarde, R.J. - 1983 - *Demographic parameters of the feral cat Felis catus population at Marion Island* - S. Afr. J. Wildl. Res. 13 (1): 10-16

Kleiman, D.G. & Eisenberg, J.F. - 1973 - *Comparisons of canid and felid social systems from an evolutionary perspective* - Anim. Behav. 21: 637

Laundré J. - 1977 - *The daytime behaviour of domestic cats in a free roaming population* - Anim. Behav., 25, 990-998

Macdonald, D.W. - 1983 - *The ecology of carnivore social behaviour* - Nature 301: 379-383

MacDonald, D.W. & Apps, P.J. - 1978 - *The social behaviour of semi-dependent farm cats (Felis catus): a progress report* - Carnivore Genetic Newsletter 3: 256-268

Messent, P.R. and Serpell, J.A. - 1981 - *An historical and biological view of the pet-owner bond* - Interrelations Between People and Pets, ed. by Foyle (Charles C. Thomas, Springsfield, Illinois), 5-22

Leyhausen, P. - *Cat Behaviour: The Predatory and Social Behaviour of Domestic and Wild Cats* - Garland STPM Press, New York, 1979

Liberg, O. - *Predation and Social Behaviour in a Population of Domestic Cat. An Evolutionary Perspective* - Ph. D. thesis, University of Lund, 1979

Robinson, R. - *Genetics for Cat Breeders*-2nd edition - Pergamon Press, Oxford, 1977

The Encyclopaedia of Mammals: vol. 1 Edited by Dr. David Macdonald - George Allen & Unwin, London, Sydney, 1984.

Natoli, E. - 1985 - *Spacing pattern of a colony of urban stray cats (Felis catus L.) in the centre of Rome* - Appl. Anim. Behav. Sci. 14: 289-304

Natoli, E. - 1985 - *Behavioural responses of urban feral cats to different types of urine marks* - Behaviour 94 (3/4): 234-243

Natoli, E. - 1985 - *Il comportamento sociale del gatto randagio (Felis catus L.) nell'ambiente urbano* - Animalia 12 (1/3): 59-85

Schaller, G.B. - *The Serengeti lion* - Univ. of Chicago Press, Chicago, 1972

Picture sources:

Mondadori Archives, 9, 10, 11, 12, 13, 15, 18, 19, 25
Cats (programme from the musical), 21
Felix by Pat Sullivan, 23
Hanna and Barbera, 23
Krazy Kat by George Herriman, 22
Steinlen, 23
The Cat Sold it, Crown Publishers Inc.

Drawings:

Carlo Giordana: 118, 120, 121, 123, 125, 129, 130, 133, 136, 137, 143, 164, 165, 166
Cecilia Giovannini: 16, 18, 22, 23, 24, 28, 29, 30, 31, 32, 33, 34, 35
Valeria Matricardi: 26, 28, 29, 30, 31, 32, 38, 39, 41, 45, 46, 53, 88, 137
Andreina Scanu: 44, 119, 122, 124, 125, 126, 127, 128, 129, 130, 131, 132, 133, 134, 135, 138, 139, 140, 141, 142, 143

Photographs by Eugenia Natoli.